THE ARCHAEOLOGY OF PROTESTANT LANDSCAPES

Archaeology of the American South: New Directions and Perspectives

Series Editor

Christopher B. Rodning

Editorial Advisory Board

Robin A. Beck

John H. Blitz

I. Randolph Daniel Jr.

Kandace R. Hollenbach

Patrick C. Livingood

Tanya M. Peres

Thomas J. Pluckhahn

Mark A. Rees

Amanda L. Regnier

Sissel Schroeder

Lynne P. Sullivan

Ian Thompson

Richard A. Weinstein

Gregory D. Wilson

THE ARCHAEOLOGY OF PROTESTANT LANDSCAPES

REVEALING THE FORMATION OF COMMUNITY IDENTITY IN THE US SOUTH

KIMBERLY PYSZKA

The University of Alabama Press
Tuscaloosa

The University of Alabama Press
Tuscaloosa, Alabama 35487-0380
uapress.ua.edu

Copyright © 2023 by the University of Alabama Press
All rights reserved.

A Dan Josselyn Memorial Publication

Inquiries about reproducing material from this work should be addressed to the University of Alabama Press.

Typeface: Minion Pro

Cover image: St. Luke's Episcopal Church, Old Cahawba, Alabama; photograph by Kimberly Pyszka
Cover design: Sandy Turner Jr.

Cataloging-in-Publication data is available from the Library of Congress.
ISBN: 978-0-8173-2162-8
E-ISBN: 978-0-8173-9456-1

In memory of Jim Pyszka (1938–2022) and
Dr. Charles H. Faulkner (1937–2022)

Contents

List of Illustrations	ix
Preface	xi
Acknowledgments	xiii
Introduction: Religious Landscapes and Material Expressions of Ideology	1
Chapter 1. St. Paul's Parish Church, South Carolina	19
Chapter 2. St. Luke's Episcopal Church, Cahaba, Alabama	47
Chapter 3. Cane Hill College, Cane Hill, Arkansas	72
Chapter 4. Forming Communities and Identities	95
Epilogue: Today's Religious Landscapes	108
Notes	113
References Cited	115
Index	127

Illustrations

Figures

I.1. Locations of the three case studies discussed in the book	3
1.1. Location of St. Paul's Parish Church ruins within the College of Charleston's Stono River Preserve	26
1.2. Ground-penetrating radar (GPR)–generated image of St. Paul's churchyard	27
1.3. Map of the St. Paul's Parish Church site	35
1.4. Units 13 and 15 indicating portion of church aisle with surrounding brick floor	36
1.5. Conceptual layout of original 1707 St. Paul's Parish Church	38
1.6. Conceptual layout of post-1720s St. Paul's Parish Church	38
1.7. Exterior and interior of Strawberry Chapel	41
1.8. Exterior and interior of St. James's (Goose Creek) Church, 2012	42
2.1. 1854 St. Luke's Episcopal Church in its current location at Old Cahawba Archaeological Park	48
2.2. Drawing of St. Luke's Episcopal Church, 1872	53
2.3. Interior of St. Luke's Episcopal Church	55
2.4. Archaeological excavations at the original site of St. Luke's Episcopal Church, 1986	66
2.5. Original map of the town of Cahawba	68
3.1. Cane Hill College 1886 building, 2017	73
3.2. Students and professors pose for a photograph in front of the 1858 Cane Hill College building	78
3.3. Sketch of the 1868 wood-framed Cane Hill College building	79
3.4. Photograph (ca. 1900) of the 1886 Cane Hill College building	80
3.5. Early twentieth-century view of Cane Hill, facing northwest	81
3.6. Distribution of all historic artifacts recovered from survey	85

3.7. Distribution of all flat glass recovered from survey	86
3.8. Distribution of all nails recovered from survey	86
4.1. Early to mid-twentieth-century school	104
E.1. Washington, DC, Temple of the Church of Jesus Christ of Latter-day Saints	110

Table

1.1. South Carolina Anglican churches and chapels constructed prior to 1725	31

Preface

Ever since I was a child, church architecture has fascinated me. My earliest memories of attending services were at my mom's family church, the United Methodist Church in Illinois City, Illinois. Besides the stained-glass windows, the church's interior was rather simple and reflected the small, rural, farming community. Its appearance stood in contrast to St. Pius, the Catholic church "in town" that I would attend on occasion with my dad's family. I would be in awe of St. Pius's overall size, the wall-sized stained-glass windows that wrapped around half the sanctuary, the large pipe organ behind the altar, and the various statues and other iconography I was not used to at the Methodist church we normally attended. Eventually, my parents, sister, and I converted to Catholicism, and while we regularly attended our "home" church of St. Patrick's, we occasionally attended mass at one of the area's several other Catholic churches. Although they had the same general features, they varied greatly in their overall design. While some tended toward the minimalistic, with clean, modern lines, others approached the grand scale and ornate features of Catholic churches I saw on television or in books. I always wondered why they appeared so different, not only differing from the Methodist church of my mom's family but also showing great variety among themselves.

My curiosity about church architecture and design only grew during the years that I studied at the College of Charleston, in Charleston, South Carolina. Nicknamed "the Holy City," Charleston has over 400 churches, many of whose steeples are among the tallest features of the skyline. I spent hours walking through churchyards and admiring the architecture and design of many of Charleston's churches. With such a concentration of places of worship, the differences in their visual appearances were obvious. But, again, I wondered why.

Over the years, my interests expanded beyond the buildings themselves and into the churchyards and broader landscapes surrounding them. Through my research, I found an answer to the question of why churches varied so much: it is because churches, as well as other types of religious structures, and the cultural landscapes they are part of, are symbols that communicate messages. This book explores some of those intended messages, specifically examining how religious organizations intentionally use landscapes and architecture to materially express their ideology, goals, and identity. Additionally, I investigate how these deliberate decisions intentionally and unintentionally affect the various communities represented either within the church itself or in the larger geographic community.

Acknowledgments

A PROJECT OF this scale is not a solo endeavor. A number of individuals and institutions who provided assistance and support deserve acknowledgments and my sincere thanks. Faculty, staff, and students affiliated with the University of Tennessee's Department of Anthropology provided guidance, funding opportunities, administrative support, and assistance with lab processing of artifacts. My peers Eleanor Breen, Stephen Carmody, Erik Johanson, Shannon Koerner, and Robert Lassen traveled to Charleston to assist with fieldwork. The College of Charleston (CofC), my undergraduate alma mater, provided me with the opportunity to conduct fieldwork at their Stono River Preserve, then called Dixie Plantation. I cannot thank enough the faculty and staff of CofC's Department of Sociology and Anthropology for their support, especially in recruiting students to assist with fieldwork at St. Paul's Parish Church. Along with the CofC Foundation, the department also provided housing and other financial assistance. Department faculty, many of whom had been my undergraduate professors, were always there for much-appreciated advice, guidance, and emotional support. It is always nice to go "home." Finally, I must thank Barney Holt with the CofC Foundation for his support and for figuratively and literally "blazing the trail" for my research at the Stono River Preserve. In Arkansas, Bobby R. Braly, former executive director of Historic Cane Hill Inc., served as my co–field director and arranged for housing, other travel-related expenses, lab space, and access to archival materials. Linda Derry, the park manager and archaeologist at Old Cahawba Archaeological Park, graciously provided access to archival documents and shared information related to her archaeological excavations and other research on St. Luke's Episcopal Church. Auburn University at Montgomery (AUM) provided faculty grants and other funding, as well as the necessary time for me to work on this book.

Staff from several archives also assisted with the research that informs this work. These institutions include the South Carolina Historical Society, the South Carolina Room at the Charleston County Public Library, CofC Addlestone Library Special Collections, Old Cahawba Archaeological Park, Cane Hill Museum, University of Arkansas Special Collections, Arkansas State Archives, and Roberts Library of Arkansas History and Art. I will always remember one individual in particular. Cynthia Hurd, a part-time librarian at CofC's Addlestone Library, assisted me multiple times with locating materials and finding ways for me to check out materials, even at times when I was not officially affiliated with CofC. A few years later, on June 17, 2015, Ms. Hurd was one of nine people shot and killed at the Mother Emanuel AME Church in Charleston. I will never forget her smile, thoughtfulness, and assistance.

There are a few others that I would like to specially mention and thank for their guidance, support, and mentorship. Barbara Heath, professor of anthropology at the University of Tennessee, oversaw my research at St. Paul's and continues to be my mentor, colleague, and friend. Her insight and ways of thinking about past landscapes influenced and guided my own study of these sites. She also taught me to think differently about what can be said about the archaeological record and other forms of material culture. Barbara's guidance, feedback, and vast knowledge of historical archaeological literature were invaluable and continue to shape my research and writing today. For over twenty years, Martha Zierden, curator of historical archaeology at the Charleston Museum, has been my "go-to" source of knowledge related to historical archaeology in general and Lowcountry archaeology and history specifically. In the early days of my research at St. Paul's, Martha and I had several discussions about potential research questions and how my research could help fill in gaps in our understanding of early colonial South Carolina. She also visited the site on multiple occasions, offering advice and providing feedback. Both Barbara and Martha instilled in me confidence not only in my research but also in my writing and, ultimately, gave me the assurance to move forward with this book. Maureen Hays, professor of anthropology at the College of Charleston, first introduced me to the Stono River Preserve property and the potential of conducting research on it. Maureen worked endlessly in recruiting students to assist with fieldwork at St. Paul's and is my co-director on all archaeological research projects at the Stono River Preserve. In her various administrative positions at CofC, Maureen promoted our research and aided in acquiring funding to support it. Her partnership in the field, on conference presentations, and in writing several publications has been an integral part of my success as a researcher. Additionally, Maureen's guidance throughout my academic career has been invaluable. Finally,

Robert Morrissey, formerly with the University of Tennessee and later associate professor of history at the University of Illinois, first introduced me to the history and study of frontiers. His guidance in the early years of my research greatly influenced its ultimate trajectory.

I must thank the numerous field school students who assisted over the years. While there are too many to name them all individually, a few stand out due to their in-depth contributions to my study of St. Paul's Parish Church, its parsonage, and the Stono River Preserve: Nate Fulmer, Casey Jenkins Jeffers, Lizzie Laforgia, Kalen McNabb, and Chase Murphree. Auburn University at Montgomery students Codie Davies, Kaylyn Decker, Nick Long, and Summer Salter assisted with the archaeological survey of the Cane Hill College site.

Excerpts from previously published articles appear in this book with permission. Selected text from "'Built for the Publick Worship of God, according to the Church of England': Anglican Landscapes and Colonialism in South Carolina," *Historical Archaeology* 47, no. 4 (2013): 1–22, and "Anglican Church Architecture and Religious Identity in Early Colonial South Carolina," *Material Culture* 49, no. 1 (2017): 78–100, appears in chapter 1. Special thanks to Wendi Schnaufer, senior acquisitions editor at the University of Alabama Press, for her guidance during the entire process of publishing this book.

Finally, thank you to my parents for their unwavering support as I pursued my educational and career goals, even when it meant cat-sitting for weeks on end while I conducted fieldwork.

THE ARCHAEOLOGY OF PROTESTANT LANDSCAPES

Introduction

Religious Landscapes and
Material Expressions of Ideology

> We must dwell here for a few moments to intimate to you . . . how much of meaning there is . . . in a properly constructed religious edifice. . . . Wood and stone, and silver and gold, and silk and linen, and divers [*sic*] colors, are but dead, mute things, which have neither speech nor language inherent in themselves, but under the hand of the cunning craftsman and skillful artificer their voices are heard among them, each one entering into the grand harmony of their utterance, being but a louder or a softer echo of the utterances of the voice of GOD.
>
> —John Freeman Young, *Journal of the 40th Annual Council of the Protestant Episcopal Church in the Diocese of Florida*, 1883 (quoted in Smith 1995:65)

Cultural landscapes—those features on the Earth that humans have built or altered—are all around us. They comprise the spaces where we live and interact, including houses, churches, schools, various other public buildings, and the numerous other types of constructed structures. They include the roads, bridges, sidewalks, and other transport networks that connect us. They are the yards, gardens, and fields where food and craft production occur. Cultural landscapes also encompass the parks, sport fields and arenas, restaurants and bars, and other places where we socialize. When one stops to consider the various aspects of the cultural landscape, it is easy to understand why archaeologist James Deetz called landscape the largest artifact that archaeologists could study (1990:4).

There is much more to landscapes than just the physical spaces and features we can visually observe. But how often do we stop to think about *why* they look the way they do? Do we consider who created and designed the landscapes that surround us or why they chose to place buildings or other cultural landscape features in specific places or facing certain directions? Why did they select certain architectural designs and features over others? Cultural landscapes have never been created or modified haphazardly. As cultural constructs, they both intentionally and unintentionally reflect the cultural practices and specific intentions of their designers and are thus full of meaning. While it may be relatively easy to interpret the intended meaning of contemporary landscapes—or at least understand the factors determining why buildings, roads, and other landscape features were placed where they are—the task is often more difficult with past landscapes. To better comprehend them, it is necessary to understand the social, political, and economic contexts at the time of their creation. Like today's cultural landscapes, those in the past were experienced by people through the various activities that they either partook in themselves or witnessed others doing. Depending on the person's background, they may have experienced a particular landscape differently than others. Therefore, to truly understand a cultural landscape, it is important to understand the various activities that took place within it (Vergunst et al. 2012:1).

In this book, I explore cultural landscapes with a focus on eighteenth- and nineteenth-century Protestant religious landscapes and structures in the southeastern United States. My primary goal is to demonstrate how past religious institutions utilized and modified natural landscape features to create cultural landscapes that materially expressed their ideology, identity, goals, and social, religious, and sometimes even political power. Where those structures were constructed, how they sat on the landscape, their architectural style, and their overall visual appearance were not random choices. Instead, they were well-thought-out and deliberate decisions made by religious leaders for the benefit of their respective religious organization, their communities, and on occasion themselves personally. A secondary goal is to show the social roles religious organizations played in the development of communities. For this purpose, I examine how landscape decisions were both intentionally and unintentionally used to unite people, often of differing religious backgrounds. In so doing, religious organizations contributed to the creation of new common identities among people living in new and still developing settlements, aiding in community formation. Finally, I want readers to reflect on today's religious landscapes and the ways they are still used to express religious, social, and political ideology and identity. Whether or not we are conscious of this fact, we continue to be shaped by religious landscapes and structures.

I discuss three case studies—St. Paul's Parish Church in South Carolina, St. Luke's Episcopal Church in Central Alabama, and Cane Hill College in Northwest Arkansas (Figure I.1). These examples date from the early eighteenth century to the turn of the twentieth century and span from the Atlantic Coast to the Ozark Mountains at the western edge of what is often considered the geographic Southeast. They represent three different Protestant organizations—the Church of England (also referred to as the Anglican Church), the Protestant Episcopal Church, and the Cumberland Presbyterian Church. The social, political, and economic conditions surrounding each community also varied. When St. Paul's Parish Church was constructed in 1707, the South Carolina colony was barely 30 years old. Tensions and

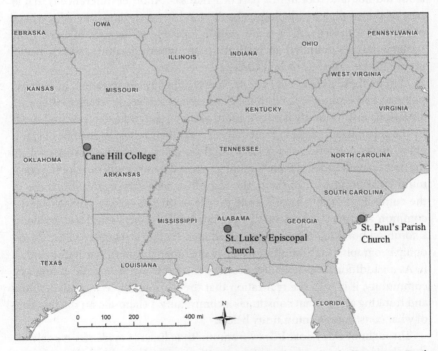

FIGURE I.1. Locations of the three case studies discussed in the book. (Base map: Esri's ArcMap; Kimberly Pyszka.)

conflict with Indigenous peoples threatened the colony's survival, and its reliance on enslaved labor to support the developing plantation economy was still in its infancy. Nearly 150 years later, construction of St. Luke's Episcopal Church began in the growing town of Cahaba, Alabama. While still a relatively young community, Cahaba and its white residents were very prosperous, accumulating their wealth from the labor of the enslaved people who cultivated the surrounding cotton fields. By this time the South's plantation economy and reliance on slavery was well established; relations with the Indigenous population were no longer a point of tension, as groups had been forced out of the region. However, another threat to Cahaba loomed as the nation teetered on the brink of civil war. Meanwhile, American expansion moved westward as the United States acquired more land from American Indians. In the northwest portion of the recently appropriated Arkansas Territory, Cumberland Presbyterians founded the community of Cane Hill in 1827. Agriculture and the related mill industry dominated the area economically, but unlike South Carolina, Alabama, and many other parts of the South, the large-size plantation economy and large-scale reliance on enslaved labor did not take root in this part of Arkansas. Another difference is that as part of their religious ideology, Cumberland Presbyterians saw educational pursuits as a priority. As a result, within a couple of decades of Cane Hill's settlement, they founded an institution of higher education, which would eventually be called Cane Hill College.

Despite these differences in time, space, religious organization, and social, political, and economic conditions, all three case studies demonstrate the ways a religious institution used one or more of their structures to create and modify the cultural landscape to materially express their religious and social ideologies, power, influence, and goals. In all three cases, I examine the sites within the first three decades of their founding, when they were still developing communities. Within each of them, the respective religious organization's use of the cultural landscape helped unite people of diverse backgrounds around a common identity. Ultimately, this provided parishioners and local residents a common bond to sculpt a new, shared identity that strengthened the developing geographic community, as well as the other communities found within it. As an additional note, while I describe each of these three case studies as a community, it is with the realization that there are multiple ways of defining and thinking about what constitutes a community. I elaborate on my thinking of what constitutes a community below.

Throughout this book, I draw from multiple lines of evidence, namely archaeological survey and excavations, artifact analysis, archival research, and architectural information on religious structures. Archaeological excavations are at the forefront of this study and play a key role in my findings and interpretations. They are particularly important to my studies of St. Paul's Parish Church and the 1850s Cane Hill College, as there is no aboveground evidence of either structure's existence. Additionally, there are few, if any, photographs, drawings, or other documentary evidence from which to extrapolate their visual appearance. At St. Paul's Parish Church, remote sensing in the form of ground-penetrating radar (GPR) testing also contributed greatly to the study. This technology provided architectural details that would not have otherwise been gained without a more expensive, time-consuming, and destructive full-scale excavation of the church ruins. While useful in studying archaeological sites in general, remote sensing techniques can be especially beneficial in studying churches as it helps archaeologists to see "hidden evidence" such as wall paintings, architectural and construction features that have been covered over time, or as in the case of St. Paul's, the entire footprint of the church below the ground surface (Brooke 1986:210; Rodwell 2005:126–127).

Furthermore, although below-ground excavations are at the heart of archaeological research, it is not limited to them, especially when considering cultural landscapes. Standing structures, ruins of former buildings, proximity to natural or cultural landscape features, and a variety of other aboveground evidence often prove to be just as important, if not more important, than the ceramics, nails, bottle glass, pipes, and other artifacts recovered from below the ground surface. Therefore, I also studied various aboveground landscape features when they were available. The most informative were extant structures, including early eighteenth-century Anglican churches in South Carolina, the 1886 Cane Hill College building, and the reassembled St. Luke's Episcopal Church. I also considered proximity to waterways and elevation from my observations of today's landscape, modern-day satellite imagery (primarily Google Earth), and historic and topographic maps. When available, historic documents and photographs also proved to be very helpful. These were especially important in Cane Hill and Cahaba, where decades of research by scholars and individuals interested in their own family histories have produced archival collections comprising photographs, maps, and a variety of primary and secondary documents. This combination of archaeological excavations and research into extant structures and other aboveground features, in conjunction with historical documents, aids in telling the larger story behind the creation and modification of past landscapes.

WHY STUDY RELIGIOUS SITES?

Sacred places can be found anywhere that has spiritual significance to an individual or a group of people (Carmichael et al. 1994). While sacred places are most often associated with religious meaning, they can also include sites that commemorate or mark a historical event. For example, places of historical significance such as Elmina Castle in Ghana or Ground Zero in New York City are considered sacred sites, especially to those whose ancestors passed through Elmina's gate or who lost family and friends at the World Trade Center on September 11, 2001. Natural landscapes such as creeks or rock formations may also serve as sacred places; Uluru (Ayers Rock) in Australia and Devils Tower in Wyoming are just two examples of natural rock formations considered to be sacred sites by Indigenous populations. At the same time, although certainly the landscapes discussed in this book can be referred to as sacred sites, I use the term *religious sites*. The reason for doing so is that the landscapes are directly associated with their respective religious organization and designed to express religious beliefs of that group.

Religious sites have much to contribute to our understanding of both past and present, due to the impact and influence of religion in the daily lives of significant segments of the population. Yet, defining what constitutes a religious site can be problematic. Today, places of worship such as churches, synagogues, temples, and mosques associated with major organized religions are easily recognizable, even to people who do not identify to that particular religion. Cemeteries, gardens, and other landscape features surrounding such places of worship are also fairly obviously identifiable religious sites.

While I recognize the variety of religious sites in this study, my research interests lay in religious structures, namely churches, as they provide information about the buildings themselves, the religious organizations they belonged to, and to the religious and social ideology of the communities they belong. While archaeologists study churches and other religious sites around the world, as a discipline church archaeology has some of its deepest roots in England. Early interest in recording churches and cemeteries centered on the recovery of remains of certain royal and religious leaders deemed important to English history. As the discipline developed in the second half of the twentieth century, church archaeologists shifted their research focus to church architecture. Through a combination of archaeological excavations and stratigraphic study of extant architectural features, archaeologists both in England and elsewhere have addressed questions related to architectural styles and plans, the various materials and techniques used in construction, and modifications made to the structure over time (Gilchrist 2014; Rodwell 2005). By studying architectural material culture, church archaeologists have examined changes in religious ideology and practices, such as those represented by murals or stained-glass windows (or lack thereof). Doctrinal changes often resulted in changes in religious material culture, especially to church architecture and interior furnishings. For example, in England, these changes were most evident during the Reformation. Pre-Reformation Catholic churches had elaborate decorations, including stained-glass windows and painted murals on the walls, while architectural features emphasized the separateness of priests and their parishioners. After the Reformation, Protestant churches and their furnishings were far less elaborate, with little, if any, interior division.

More recently, church archaeologists have turned to other areas of research beyond church architecture and construction. For example, petrographic analysis of tile, glass, and marble has been used to inform archaeologists of trade networks and, therefore, transportation routes for materials used in church construction. English churchyard studies provide information about demography, genealogy, and ritual practices among congregations (Morris 1983). The introduction of geographic information systems led to the ability for archaeologists to better map changes to religious landscapes on a regional scale, as well as over time, allowing for a better understanding of how religious groups shaped the development of the land, including local communities. Now archaeologists can ask additional questions that relate to agency, identity construction, differing perspectives, and various religious practices (Gilchrist 2014).

For their part North American historical archaeologists have often shied away from the study of churches, churchyards, and religious organizations. Veit et al. (2009:3–4) provide a number of reasons for this lack of research into churches and cemeteries. First, due to the amount of documentary evidence related to religious institutions, there is often the mistaken belief that everything to be learned from them can be found in documents. Second, religious sites rarely fall under Section 106 of the National Historic Preservation Act of 1966 mandating archaeological survey and, therefore, are not protected under the act. A third possible reason is the belief that churches and cemeteries do not contribute to a better understanding of the past. Finally, according to Veit et al., many archaeologists are less interested in studying the religious and spiritual beliefs of past people than they are in other areas of inquiry because they are unquantifiable.

In more recent years, though, there has been a shift. Increasing numbers of archaeologists are interested in studying churches and other religious sites as there is an increased awareness of how they are able to contribute to questions of identity, consumerism, trade, and colonialism (Veit et al. 2009). The main difficulty that archaeologists who study churches and other religious sites face is the general lack of objects that people used in their everyday lives (Harpole et al. 2007; Ward and McCarthy 2009). Artifact assemblages from church sites tend to be largely architectural in nature, comprised primarily of bricks, mortar, window glass, and nails. I faced these same difficulties in archaeological research at the St. Paul's Parish Church site (Pyszka 2012), a Methodist church site in Cane Hill (Pyszka et al. 2018), and the Cane Hill College site discussed in chapter 3. To address this issue, other forms of material culture that can also express religious and social beliefs need to be examined, such as the churchyard and associated buildings that surround many churches. Therefore, studying churches, and religious sites in general, through the lens of landscape archaeology, is beneficial in that it can provide insight into the thought processes behind the use and design of religious sites.

APPROACHES TO LANDSCAPE ARCHAEOLOGY AND ARCHITECTURAL STUDIES

A common thread that spans the three case studies in this book is that past religious leaders created and modified the cultural landscape, including their choice of architectural style and features, to express their religious beliefs and various types of power. As mentioned, an archaeological study focused on landscape and architecture is particularly useful in studying religious organizations and their structures due to their artifact assemblages typically containing very few nonarchitectural artifacts. As forms of material culture, landscapes and architecture also express cultural practices and beliefs. By examining them, especially in combination, we can learn more about the cultural and ideological reasons *why* people shaped their landscapes and designed their buildings the ways they did. This combined approach is especially important when studying landscapes and buildings created in the past 500 years or so, as landscapes provide the "solid foundation on which the architectural monument is erected and the scenic background against which it is displayed or 'set off' to best advantage" (Ingold 2012:205).

Archaeological approaches to studying the cultural landscape have evolved throughout the past several decades, in tandem with the study of material culture in general. In the 1950s and 1960s, Julian Steward's ideas of cultural ecology stressed the interactions between past humans and their environment (1955). Cultural practices and change were thought to be simply responses to one's environment. Such ecological approaches regarding how natural landscapes shaped everyday life and attempts to reconstruct past environment conditions can be considered the first studies in what would later become known as landscape archaeology (Patterson 2008:78). With the beginnings of processual archaeology in the 1950s, archaeologists began to think about landscapes in relation to settlement patterns. For Gordon Willey (1953:1), this approach included how humans organized themselves on the landscape, as well as their structures, spatial patterning, and social interactions. Studies of "settlement archaeology" continued well into the 1960s and beyond (Chang 1968). While studies of settlement patterns are still a part of the archaeological study of landscapes in North America (Crass and Brooks 1997; Hartley 1984; Lewis 1984; South and Hartley 1980), historical archaeologists have begun to examine other aspects of cultural landscapes, namely, what their creators and designers were trying to express through their modification and use.

Since the 1980s, when landscape studies gained popularity among North American historical archaeologists, critical materialism functioned as a leading theoretical approach in discussing landscapes and how they are modified to express power. Building on the ideas of Marx, critical materialists believe that studies of the past should be grounded in the rise and development of capitalism. In regard to landscapes, research in this vein has often focused on how various historical actors have modified the landscape in order to express their power and social status and to mask the ideological conflicts stemming from the inequality between classes (Delle 1998, 1999; Epperson 1990; Leone 2005; Leone et al. 2005). Mark Leone's (1984) study of William Paca's eighteenth-century Annapolis garden is a hallmark example of this approach. He states that Paca and other mid-eighteenth-century elites designed their gardens to mask the contradictions of their lives—namely that while they promoted revolutionary ideas of liberty, their wealth and status were based on enslaved labor. By manipulating nature through experimenting with grouping, breeding, and transplanting trees and other plants, manipulating plane geometry to create illusions of the garden's depth, and frequently referring to antiquity in the landscape, Paca expressed his control over nature. Per Leone, by doing so, Paca naturalized his role in society and created a past for it.

A primary criticism of Leone's ideas of critical materialism is that it assumes that subordinate groups were persuaded by elite constructions of the landscape rather than examining how they viewed, interpreted, and negotiated that landscape (De Cunzo and Ernstein 2006:261). Many researchers, including myself, continue to base their research questions on the idea that landscapes were used by elites or others in power positions as one way to represent their social, economic, and political power. However, interpretations should also be based on the realization that subordinate groups contributed to the landscape as well, and that relationships between elite and subordinate classes could be negotiated.

Today, many archaeologists who study historical landscapes, including the design choices made regarding architectural styles, ask questions about the intended social, racial, political, religious, economic, and personal meanings that a given landscape's creators and designers attempted to express through its modification and use (De Cunzo and Ernstein 2006; Deetz 1990; Delle 1998, 1999; Epperson 1990; Heath 2007, 2010; Heath and Lee 2010; Leone 1984; Leone et al. 2005; Proebsting and Gary 2016; Yamin and Metheny 1996; Young 2000; Zierden and Stine 1997). Specific to religious landscapes, archaeologists, architectural historians, and art historians have shown that, by studying religious landscapes and buildings, we can learn about expressions of religious ideology (Bromberg and Shepard 2006; De Cunzo et al. 1996; Kryder-Reid 1994, 1996; Scharfenberger 2009), religious and social identity (Baugher and Veit 2014; Hawkins 1983; Kruczek-Aaron 2015), and religious and social power (Arendt 2011; Lenik 2010, 2011; Lydon 2009; Nelson 2001, 2008; Upton 1986).

My own ways of thinking about past landscapes, architectural styles, and what we can learn from them have largely been shaped by many of these ideas. In particular, my research and interpretations have been greatly influenced by DeMarrais et al.'s (1996) concept of the "materialization of ideology," which is rooted in a materiality approach. Studies from this vantage point examine various attributes of objects, how people use their agency to interact with them, and how they are shaped by their experiences with those objects, structures, and other forms of material culture (DeMarrais et al. 2004:1). A materiality approach is particularly useful when studying religion, as nearly all religious groups use material objects in a variety of forms. Artwork, iconography, beads, amulets, vestments, and architecture and landscapes are just some examples of material items religious groups use to express their beliefs, ideas, and traditions while also relying on them to legitimate their authority and power (Droogan 2013:1).

DeMarrais et al. view ideology as a source of power, specifically social power, that is materially expressed through tangible types of material culture, such as ceremonial events, symbolic objects, public monuments and landscapes, and even writing (1996:15–16). For this study, I focus on their discussion of landscapes and public monuments, which includes churches and related landscapes. According to DeMarrais et al., leaders of dominant groups construct public monuments and landscapes to build and promote group unity and cohesion, stake their claim to land, and to convey power—not just those that belong to their group but also to people who belong to less dominant groups (1996:18–19). From the Church of England in early eighteenth-century South Carolina, to mid-nineteenth-century Episcopalians in Central Alabama, to mid to late nineteenth-century Cumberland Presbyterians in Northwest Arkansas, I argue that religious organizations have shaped the cultural landscape for these same reasons—to claim the land, reinforce and display their religious, social, and, when applicable, political power and authority, and to promote a sense of unity through a shared identity.

An examination of materialization often begins with providing a description of what an object—or building in this case—symbolizes. However, there needs to be more to such an examination. To start, we can also ask questions about intended messages and functions, identity, and beliefs (DeMarrais 2004:13). Therefore, in addition to describing St. Paul's Parish Church, St. Luke's Episcopal Church, Cane Hill College, and their respective surrounding landscapes based on archaeological and/or architectural evidence, I examine how they visually expressed the beliefs of each religious organization, the possible intended messages and audiences of their designers and creators, and how these structures were material expressions of identity. Furthermore, I consider the responses people had to these planned and designed religious landscapes and buildings, namely how landscape decisions by religious leaders led to the formation of new community identities or the strengthening of ones already in place.

As historical archaeology is inherently interdisciplinary, scholars from other disciplines have influenced my study as well. Similar to recent trends in historical archaeology, many art historians and architectural historians have moved beyond providing general descriptions of objects to search for their cultural and social meaning(s). For example, art historian Harriett Hawkins (1983) examined rural South Carolina Anglican churches to study their role in maintaining and expressing English culture. By continuing London-style church architecture, builders ensured that parishioners felt more connected to England. This connection also helped preserve English identity, as parishioners were able to present themselves as being wealthy and sophisticated, even though they were living in the relatively isolated South Carolina colony. Likewise, architectural historian Dell Upton (1986) searched for meaning in the layout of Virginia's eighteenth-century Anglican churches and the movement of people through the landscapes that surrounded them, concentrating on the ways that churches reflected and upheld Virginia's social distinctions. In a similar fashion, art historian Louis Nelson (2001, 2008) discussed how Anglican material culture, including architecture, use of landscape, interior furnishings, and gravestones, represented eighteenth-century thinking and reflected broader social changes. Specifically, Nelson argued that South Carolina's Anglican leaders purposely used church architecture and landscape to illustrate their presence and power in the religiously tolerant colony, an idea that greatly influenced my work at St. Paul's Parish Church. Although these examples are limited to the eighteenth-century Anglican Church in South

Carolina and Virginia, their ideas and interpretations can also be applied to religious landscapes from other religious organizations and time periods.

While understanding the deliberate meanings is an essential part of interpreting cultural landscapes, it is just as important to ask questions about how the intended audiences viewed those same landscapes. Did they find the meaning in landscape or architectural features to be as its creators and designers intended? Or did they view them differently, and if so, how? How people view, interpret, and understand the cultural landscapes around them is based on their personal experiences and cultural background (Chenoweth 2021; Rodman 2003:205). Johnson (2006:4) refers to landscapes as "land-scapes," meaning that they are not just the physical land, structures, and other cultural features physically on the land. Instead, they are the images our minds see when viewing landscapes. In short, individuals will envision the landscape in their own ways, depending on their land-scape.

An example of these two distinctive viewpoints of landscape, one physical and the other mental, can be seen in how the words "space" and "place" are used by landscape scholars. *Space* refers to any area—a room, a building, or an open area, just to name a few examples. *Place* refers to a socially constructed space that expresses cultural meaning and is experienced by an individual or a group (Casey 2008; Low and Lawrence-Zúñiga 2003; Pauls 2006; Ryden 1993). Therefore, any area is a space, but it is a *place* only to those who ascribe specific meaning to that *space*. As places are experienced by individuals, they often hold different meanings for different people, determined by their specific experience with that place. Churches and other types of religious landscapes are physical *spaces*, but they are also *places* that convey meaning, hold memories, and are experienced, even by people who do not belong to that particular religious organization (Morris 1989:3).

Therefore, I fully acknowledge that not everyone viewed and experienced the religious landscapes I discuss in the three case studies at the heart of this book in the ways their creators intended. Using Johnson's terminology, their "land-scapes" were different. The less dominant groups, who were the intended audiences of the material expressions of ideology, did not necessarily accept the messages as intended. In fact, they often resisted them. Sometimes this resistance was more open, such as seen in South Carolina when the Yamasee Indians attacked English traders, igniting the Yamasee Indian War, or when enslaved peoples rebelled against their owners in the Stono Rebellion of 1739. Most of the time, though, less dominant groups resisted in more subtle ways, such as through the persistence of their traditional cultural practices and/or through the continuation or even strengthening of their own community identities. Still, my focus here is on the landscape decisions made by religious institutions and how those landscapes were material expressions of religious and social ideologies. Those religious institutions were controlled by white, European American men, as were the leaders of the individual churches within those institutions. Therefore, I focus my study and interpretations more on their ideology and the messages they intended, and to a lesser extent on how those messages were received by others.

COMMUNITY IDENTITY

In general, archaeologists define a community as a dynamic social unit comprised of nonrelated people who interact within a particular space or place and who share similar life experiences and/or cultural identifiers (Isbell 2000:243; Yaeger and Canuto 2000:5; Zierden 2002:182). In their review of the various approaches that ethnographers, sociologists, and other scholars have used in community studies research, Yaeger and Canuto (2000:2) identified four theoretical perspectives—structural-functionalist, historical-developmental, ideational, and interactional. My approach to community studies most closely matches the ideational perspective as they define it, while sharing aspects of the interactional one. An ideational perspective centers on identity—those traits and characteristics that an individual sees as linking oneself to a specific group of people, as well as those that separate an individual from other groups (Yaeger and Canuto 2000:1; see also Anderson 1991 and Cohen 1985). Examples of cultural identifiers that a person uses to establish their own identity include those based on ethnicity, race, age, religion, gender, and personal interests, plus a multitude of others. Interactional perspectives, largely based in practice theory, focus on how communities and community identities develop through interactions with others. More specifically, through the sharing of a physical space and regularly interacting with others within that space, an awareness of shared cultural traits is shaped and develops, leading to the formation of a community (Yaeger and Canuto 2000:5–6).

Therefore, I see communities as groups of people who have a shared, common identity. While that identity can be linked to a specific space or place, it is more often based on one or more cultural or social identifiers. As a result, multiple communities are typically found within a geographic community. Additionally, as identity is constructed through several cultural identifiers, it is possible, and very likely, that individuals are a part of multiple communities. For example, the Cahaba and St. Luke's Episcopal Church case study focuses on the geographic community of Cahaba, which includes all people who live, work, attend worship services, or interact in numerous other ways within the town's actual physical space and its surrounding area. However, within the geographic Cahaba community there were multiple other communities, developed through a shared identity. These communities included the Episcopalian community, the enslaved community, the Black community (comprised of both enslaved and freed people), and the white community, among others. It is also important to note that the identifiers that link members of a community are not fixed. Like all aspects of culture, they change over time, resulting in the reshaping of communities and the creation of new ones.

In this book, I also examine how a community's shared identity develops, in particular, the role of race and the process of racialization in its development. Specifically, I focus on how religious landscapes and architecture helped to create, express, shape, and reinforce racial identity—not only for individuals but also for larger communities. Although race makes up only a part of one's overall identity, it is typically interconnected with other cultural identifiers such as ethnicity, gender, and religion. However, racial identity is unique when compared to these other cultural identifiers in that it is typically defined from an outsider's perspective rather than one's own (Orser 2007:8). Through the process of racialization, socially constructed categories are created and shaped, "to identify and differentiate people who are defined variously through time by reference to selective biological differences and cultural differences in order to maintain one group's greater access to power and resources" (Gorsline 2015:292).

In my discussions of race in the formation of community identity, I draw on critical race theory (CRT), which "acknowledges, analyzes, and challenges the fundamental role of the law in the construction of racial difference and the perpetuation of racial oppression in American society" (Epperson 2004:101). Specifically, my work is guided by one area of CRT research—the study of whiteness, often referred to as critical whiteness studies. In historical archaeology, critical whiteness studies have the goal to "draw attention to how whiteness has been used as a means of social power in order to gain unfair advantage" (Gorsline 2015:293). Like Black or any other racial category, white is not a biological category. Instead, it is a social and cultural one that has been constructed and altered through racialization. However, unlike other racial categories, what it means to be white has largely been created and shaped by white people themselves, or at least those with the power to do so. Developing a white identity was important because one could not create and reinforce a Black identity, or other identifying category, without also creating a white identity (Orser 2007:39). There must be "us" to have "them." In scholarly work, as well as United States society in general, "white" and "whiteness" are typically considered to be the norm that all other racial categories are compared and measured against. In fact, it is so normal that some social scientists have discussed the "invisibility" of whiteness (Frankenburg

1993:6; Gorsline 2015:293; Lipsitz 1995:369). However, no matter how normal or invisible it seems, because the formation of white as a racial category and how it has changed over time shapes how others are racially perceived, archaeologists and other scholars of the past must not ignore either the category or what it means to be white.

In general, historical archaeologists have much to add to the study of the construction and continuation of racial identity. Especially in the United States, almost every social structure we study was created and/or has been shaped by race to some extent (Orser 2007:3). Additionally, archaeologists have a unique ability to link social meanings associated with race to material culture (Orser 2007:34). While present in all three case studies, the development and reinforcement of racial identity are most evident in my discussions of St. Paul's Parish Church and St. Luke's Episcopal Church, largely due to their location in regions where the economy relied heavily on enslaved labor and where enslaved peoples comprised a vast majority of the population. In these two case studies, I connect the creation and reinforcement of racial identity to religious landscapes, in particular the architecture style and spatial layout of religious buildings. While slavery was present in Cane Hill and Northwest Arkansas in general, and Black people were present in the community and contributed to its development, there were not the large numbers of enslaved peoples as there were in South Carolina and Alabama. Additionally, there is no mention in historical documents of Black people attending church services at any of the Cumberland Presbyterian churches in the area or attending classes in any of their schools. Therefore, in the Cane Hill case study I do not focus on the construction and development of racial identity as I did in the other two cases.

OVERVIEW OF BOOK

Chapter 1 introduces the context of early colonial South Carolina. Upon its founding in 1670, Carolina's leaders declared the colony to be religiously tolerant. Despite the Church of England being considered "the only true and orthodox" religion in the colony (Dalcho 1820:4), white Christians and Jewish settlers were welcomed. However, Carolinian religious tolerance did have some limitations, as Catholics were not. In 1706 the colony's General Assembly passed the Church Act, which formally established the Church of England, an important event in that it led to the proprietary government recognizing the Church of England as the colony's official religion and supporting it politically and monetarily (Woolverton 1984:16). The Church Act of 1706 also formed nine parishes, including St. Paul's Parish located to the west and south of Charles Town (later Charleston).

In this chapter, I contend that St. Paul's leaders purposely created a cultural landscape that materially expressed the Church of England's power and influence in the colony. They did so in two ways. First, they situated their parish church to showcase it and make it a prominent feature on the landscape. By doing so, they communicated messages of the Church's power, presence, and influence. Second, in their design choices for their individual churches, parish leaders set out to express English influence and power. Third, I argue that by using architecture to their advantage, St. Paul's leaders designed their church in order to attract the large number of Dissenters—those white settlers who did not belong to the Church of England—who lived in the parish.

In chapter 2, I turn attention to Old Cahawba, located in Central Alabama, just west of Selma. At its founding in 1818, Cahawba served as Alabama's first capital; however, only five years later, state officials moved the capital to Tuscaloosa. While the town's population and importance within the state declined, it remained the county seat of Dallas County. Beginning in the 1830s, Cahaba's (spelling changed from Cahawba) population and economy boomed, as it became a very prosperous cotton town and one of the wealthiest antebellum communities in both Alabama and in the United States more generally. At the time, Cahaba had several churches scattered through its community, including St. Luke's Episcopal Church. After the Civil War, Cahaba changed drastically, both economically and demographically: most white families, now former cotton planters, moved and the town's population declined significantly. In their place, newly freed African Americans remained or moved to the town, forming a new community. Still, despite their efforts, Cahaba continued to decline. By the 1930s, most of its residents left the town, leaving behind abandoned buildings and a few remaining families. Today, Cahaba is a virtual ghost town.

Although Cahaba had a number of churches, my discussion centers on St. Luke's Episcopal Church. Constructed in 1854, St. Luke's is where most of Cahaba's wealthiest residents, many of whom had relocated from northeastern states, worshipped. Drawing from archaeological and documentary research conducted by Old Cahawba's park manager and archaeologist Linda Derry and on the extant structure itself, I argue that Cahaba's most influential residents purposely chose its Gothic Revival architecture as a visual expression of their more sophisticated, cosmopolitan, and modern tastes. Additionally, it expressed the wealth, social status of its parishioners and those of the entire community. White Episcopalians also used architecture as a means to segregate St. Luke's Black parishioners, both enslaved and freed, reinforcing their own racial identity, while reminding Black parishioners of their status within the church and the larger Cahaba community. I also examine the landscape selection of the church to show how St. Luke's location in the heart of the town and along the banks of the Alabama River was another way for Episcopalian leaders and parishioners to materially express influence and power in the flourishing antebellum community.

Chapter 3 presents the final case study, Cane Hill College, located in northwestern Arkansas. Cumberland Presbyterians founded Cane Hill in 1827 with an identity centered on four facets of everyday life important to them—religion, education, industry, and agriculture. Since the town's inception, education played an important role in in the plans Cumberland Presbyterians had for their community, culminating in the founding of Cane Hill College. The 1886 college building still stands today and remains the visual and social center of the community. While I discuss this extant structure, my focus is on Cane Hill College as it existed in the mid-nineteenth century. Similar to the Anglican churches in early colonial South Carolina, I argue that Cumberland Presbyterian community leaders purposely situated Cane Hill College on the landscape. By placing it on "the Hill," as local residents still refer to it, they ensured town residents, visitors, and travelers saw their college. As the focal point for the community, Cane Hill College materially expressed the Cumberland Presbyterian emphasis on education, as well as its influence in the community. The surviving college building also provides a great example of how the meaning of a structure can change over time.

In the final chapter, I revisit all three case studies to explore how landscape and architecture decisions made by leaders of the relevant religious organizations influenced the development or strengthening of community identities. In so doing, these organizations aided communities to develop and prosper in varying ways. For example, in the early decades of the eighteenth century, white identity in South Carolina shifted from one based on religious differences (Anglican or Dissenter) to one based on skin color. I explore the idea that architectural decisions made by Anglican leaders helped shape this transformation of white identity. Similarly, in Cahaba, architecture and landscape decisions made at St. Luke's Episcopal Church reinforced parishioners' identity not only as Episcopalians but also as white, wealthy enslavers who lived in a modern, cosmopolitan town. Additionally, I argue that those decisions paradoxically strengthened the community of Black parishioners, which ultimately led to the continuation of the Black community of Cahaba after the white population basically abandoned the town.

Meanwhile, in Cane Hill, the formation and development of community identity took a different route. From its initial founding in 1827 through much of the nineteenth century, Cane Hill's identity centered on religion, namely the Cumberland Presbyterian Church, and education. However, over time the community's identity shifted. During the twentieth century, especially its last few decades, Cane Hill's identity shifted to remembering its history and preserving its heritage. Today, the extant 1886 college building stands at the center of the community's identity and is a symbol of historic preservation efforts and the revitalization of Cane Hill.

Although the focus of this book has been on past religious landscapes, at its conclusion, I encourage readers to reflect on present-day religious landscapes and architecture. Just like in the past, religious organizations still use landscape and architecture to express their religious ideologies and their power and influence. And they still shape our identities—as individuals and as part of a larger society.

CHAPTER ONE

St. Paul's Parish Church, South Carolina

> And be it further Enacted by the Authority aforesaid, That the commissioners hereafter named, shall have power to take up by grant from the lords proprietors, or purchase the same from them, or any other person, and have, take and receive so much land, as they shall think necessary for the several sites of the said several Churches, and the Cemeteries or Church-Yards, for the burial of Christian people there, in the several places mentioned, and shall also direct and appoint the building of the said several Churches not already built, according to such dimensions and of such materials as they shall think fitting.
>
> —South Carolina General Assembly, Church Act of 1706

In the Church Act of 1706, the South Carolina General Assembly granted Anglican commissioners the power to obtain land to build their churches upon and to establish their churchyards and cemeteries. The General Assembly also gave them the freedom to design those churches as they desired. But what attributes would the Anglican commissioners "think fitting"? Along with individual parish leaders, they had several decisions to make before construction of parish churches could even begin. Some of the items they needed to consider were the specific location where a church would be built, its architectural style, the construction materials to use, and its overall visual appearance. Whether intentional or not, their decisions regarding these considerations also expressed cultural and social meaning. As one of the Anglican churches designed and constructed during the early 1700s, St. Paul's Parish Church, originally located outside of modern-day Charleston, provides an opportunity to examine landscape and architectural decisions made by Anglican leaders and the possible messages they sent both to parishioners and anyone else who observed Anglican churches situated on the Carolina landscape.

When I began my research into St. Paul's Parish and its first church, I found very little historical information to draw from. Most of it came from a commemorative plaque placed by a women's group affiliated with the present-day St. Paul's Church in nearby Summerville, the descendant church of the original St. Paul's Parish Church. The plaque reads, "1706 St. Paul's Parish, Stono, One of the Nine Original Carolina Parishes. On this site, given by Landgrave Edmund Bellinger, a brick church 35 by 25 feet was built in 1708. The parsonage was burned by Indians in 1715. The parish was divided in 1734 and in 1746, the church was relocated 8 miles N.W. of here at Beech Hill 15 miles south of Summerville, S.C. Erected 1970."

While this plaque provided a starting point, several questions remained. Where was the church located specifically? What did it look like? What became of the structure after the church relocated to Beech Hill? Where did the St. Paul's Church women's group obtain their information? In conjunction with the College of Charleston Department of Sociology and Anthropology, I conducted archaeological and documentary research to address these and other questions.

Based on this research, in this chapter I contend that St. Paul's Parish leaders, and other leaders within the South Carolina Anglican Church, purposely shaped the cultural landscape to materially express the Church's power, presence, and influence in the developing colony. They did this by positioning their parish churches on the colonial landscape in such a way as to draw attention to them. Thereby, they made statements about the presence, power, and influence of the Church of England in the colony. They also sent another message, one that staked English claim to the land even though other European powers and local Indigenous peoples, namely the Kiawahs, Stonos, Bohickets, and Edistos, still claimed and sought control over it. Additionally, St. Paul's leaders used architecture to materially express their goals and did so to their advantage. Specifically, I argue that they designed their church to attract the large number of Presbyterians and other Dissenters, white settlers who did not belong to the Church of England, who lived in the parish. As a result, the religiously diverse white population within the parish became more unified and formed a sense of community around a new common identity, one based more on whiteness rather than on religion.

HISTORICAL OVERVIEW

As early as the sixteenth century, Europeans explored what is now South Carolina with Spain, France, and later England laying claim to the land and its presumed riches. All three countries established settlements in Carolina to stake their claim, with varying degrees of success. In 1562 the French attempted a settlement, founding Charlesfort along Port Royal Sound, near present-day Beaufort. The French settlement faced many hardships and did not survive its first year (DePratter and South 1990). In response to the failed attempt and word that the French were going to try again, in 1566 the Spanish established Santa Elena on present-day Parris Island, also on Port Royal Sound. Within three years, Santa Elena was a thriving colony, with approximately two hundred settlers living in forty houses. Although disease, food shortages, and conflict with local American Indian groups plagued the colony, Santa Elena persevered and eventually became the capital of Spanish Florida. Despite its initial success, in 1587 the Spanish abandoned Santa Elena in order to consolidate their forces in St. Augustine, a move largely due to the increasing English presence in the Port Royal area and the destruction of St. Augustine by Sir Francis Drake (Deagan 2013:365).

Nearly eighty-five years passed before another European power attempted to settle Carolina. In the 1663 Charter of Carolina, King Charles II granted the colony to eight of his most loyal supporters, the Lords Proprietors, giving them the authority to govern the colony. After a few years of planning, English colonists arrived in April 1670 and established what would become the colony's first permanent European settlement. The English located their settlement, named Charles Town in honor of Charles II, on Albemarle Point, along the west bank of the Ashley River. Ten years later, they moved the settlement across the river to Oyster Point, today's downtown Charleston.

Within fifty years of the initial English settlement, South Carolina grew to be one of the wealthiest colonies in British America. Its wealth initially came from deerskins traded by Native Americans and, later, from rice cultivated by enslaved Africans. During this period, the political atmosphere of South Carolina evolved as well. The Lords Proprietors continued to govern through their appointed governor, but over time, the colony's General Assembly gained more control and power. Beginning around the turn of the eighteenth century, the Church of England, its leaders, and followers gained more power and influence within the General Assembly and therefore, within the colony. As a result, the Church began to play more than just a religious role, increasingly influencing political decisions. Additionally, and in a fashion often unrecognized, the Church of England became an important part in the social lives of most white South Carolinians. Europeans and European Americans came together to worship at local Anglican parish churches, regardless of their religious background. The Church also played a role in the lives of non-white peoples, sending missionaries from the Society for the Propagation of the Gospel in Foreign Parts (SPG) to Carolina with the explicit goal of Christianizing non-Christians, namely Indigenous peoples and Africans. When successful, conversion allowed for greater control over the converted, while excluding those "heathens and infidels" who did not convert from the Christian community. Thus, in the outlying areas of the colony, Anglican churches and parsonages became places where English identity was upheld, and a new, white Carolina identity formed.

THE CHURCH OF ENGLAND AND THE CAROLINA COLONY

From the time of its charter in 1663, the Carolina colony was designed as a place of religious tolerance, welcoming to all Christians, except Catholics. In 1669 Lord Anthony Ashley Cooper, one of the eight Lords Proprietors and later Earl of Shaftsbury, wrote the Fundamental Constitution with the assistance of a colleague, philosopher John Locke. While the people of Carolina never officially ratified the Fundamental Constitution or its subsequent four revisions, it established the policies of the colony and the proprietary government, including religious policy (Bolton 1982; Dalcho 1820). Even though the document stressed religious tolerance, it still declared the Church of England as "the only true and orthodox" religion in the colony (Dalcho 1820:4).

Even though the Church of England was the preferred religion, due to the colony's stance on religious tolerance many members of the General Assembly, the colony's main governing body, were Dissenters. Early in the colony's history, the various denominations existed in relative peace in both the General Assembly and elsewhere, but by the turn of the eighteenth century political conflicts divided Anglicans and Dissenters. These conflicts were in large part due to growing religious and political divisions in England that were centered on the High churchmen, those who believed in a strict following of Anglican teachings, and the Low churchmen, who believed in a more Puritan religious life and were more open to religious tolerance (Bolton 1982:12). It was under the leadership of Governor Nathanial Johnson, an Anglican, that the General Assembly passed the 1706 Church Act. The act created nine parishes and called for the construction of several churches and also gave parish church supervisors the power to make decisions regarding all aspects of church construction, including site selection, design, and labor issues.

One of the parishes created by the 1706 Church Act was St. Paul's, located to the southwest of Charles Towne. During the late seventeenth century and into the early eighteenth century, this area was considered virtual wilderness with few settlers. The first settlers to the area, and others that followed, built homes and towns, and their location along the Stono River allowed them to maintain contact with Charles Towne. Initially this area attracted entrepreneurs involved in the growing Indian trade with the Yamasee and other Indian groups farther to the south (Zierden et al. 1999), while later its landscape of swamps, marshes, and tidal waters made it ideal for rice production. In the spring of 1707, construction of the St. Paul's Parish Church began on land donated by Landgrave Edmund Bellinger (Conveyance from Estate of Landgrave Bellinger, 1706, Records of St. Paul's, Stono, 1706–1864 (0273.03.32), South Carolina Historical Society, Charleston). Parish church supervisors—Robert Seabrook, Hugh Hicks, and Thomas Farr—were responsible for all aspects of the church's construction including its exact location and architectural design (St. Paul's Parish Vestry to SPG Secretary, 20 January 1715, SPG Microfilm Series B, Volume IV:41). All three men were parish residents, as well as high-ranking political figures in the colonial government. Under their guidance, the 7.62 × 10.67 m (25 × 35 ft) brick structure was completed by November of that year (St. Paul's Vestry to SPG Secretary, 20 January 1715, SPG Microfilm Series B, Volume IV:41).

In April 1715, events just to the south of St. Paul's Parish drastically altered life for St. Paul's Parish residents and all South Carolinians, as well as threatened the survival of the English colony. On April 15th of that year, a group of Yamasee Indians attacked, tortured, and killed white traders in the Yamasee town of Pocotaligo Town. Within a week, over one hundred white settlers and were killed or captured by the Yamasee (Oatis 2004:126). After this initial attack the violence subsided, but it was far from over. While the English sent men to the garrisons and hundreds of white settlers from the rural parishes fled to the relative safety of Charles Towne, the Yamasee organized an alliance of Indian groups from throughout the Southeast. In July of that year, 600–700 members of the Indian confederation moved northward in an attempt to attack Charles Towne, killing settlers and burning buildings they encountered (Oatis 2004; Ramsey 2008). As they marched through St. Paul's Parish, confederation members caused tremendous loss of life and destruction, including the St. Paul's parsonage house. Although it was only two hundred yards away from the parsonage house, St. Paul's Church was left relatively unscathed. Reverend William Bull, the assigned missionary to

St. Paul's at the time, wrote of the damage to his parsonage house, but noted that the only damage to the church was, "the breaking a few of the windows, and tearing of the Lining from one of the best Pews" (Bull to SPG Secretary, August 10, 1715, SPG Microfilm Series B, Volume IV:40–42). By late summer militia from Virginia arrived in South Carolina to assist the English and the Yamasee confederation began to fall apart, ultimately retreating to St. Augustine. From the time of the initial attack in April through the late summer, the very survival of the colony was in question and the Yamasee War marked a pivotal time in the English settlement of the Southeast. The South Carolina colony was almost lost and when considered as a proportion of the English population, the loss of over 400 settlers makes it one of the bloodiest wars on American soil (Ramsey 2008:2).

While the events of the Yamasee Indian War of 1715 led to tremendous loss of life and property damage in St. Paul's Parish, the relative peace in the years afterwards led to a dramatic rise in the parish's population. The increase of parish residents was in large part due to the marshes and waterways of the parish being especially attractive as the demand for rice in the colony grew. As the population increased, the 7.62 × 10.67 m (25 × 35 ft) church was no longer sufficient as it was overcrowded and parishioners "were forced to stand without the door, and others hang at the windows" (quoted in Dalcho 1820:352). An addition to the church was completed in 1732 and the newly expanded church sat nearly two hundred parishioners (Bull to SPG Secretary, October 10, 1722, SPG Microfilm Series B, Volume IV:240–241; Standish to SPG Secretary, June 6, 1726, SPG Microfilm Series A, Volume 14:316–317). Even with the addition, overcrowding was still an issue. To help alleviate the problem, the parish was divided in 1734 and St. John's (Colleton) Parish was created from the southern portion of St. Paul's Parish. As a consequence, St. Paul's Parish Church was no longer centrally located within the parish. In 1742, parishioners petitioned to have the more centrally located chapel of ease declared the parish church (Orr to SPG Secretary, March 31, 1742, SPG Microfilm, Letter XIII:164). Chapels of ease were secondary places of worship, often constructed so that parishioners would not have to travel as far to their parish church. In South Carolina, parish ministers usually traveled to their parish's chapel of ease once every few weeks to conduct services, while a church warden or vestryman would lead services other weeks. It is unknown when the St. Paul's chapel of ease officially became the parish church or how long services continued at the original church along the Stono, but this move must have occurred by 1756 when the original church was dismantled with material from it being removed and reused for repairs to the new parish church (Dalcho 1820:357).

Since the mid-eighteenth century when services ceased at the original St. Paul's Parish Church, the razing of the church by parishioners in 1756 and the passage of time have left very little record of the decisions made by the supervisors. The decisions of Seabrook, Hicks, and Farr, the three church supervisors at St. Paul's, were probably not made lightly, with much thought going into the placement of their church on the landscape, overall church architecture, and construction materials. The choices they made were likely influenced by their faith, political power, socioeconomic class, and goals, as well as those of their fellow parishioners and the Anglican Church. Through archaeological research, the decisions made by Seabrook, Hicks, and Farr in regard to the placement of the church on the landscape and their possible reasons for doing so can now be discussed.

ST. PAUL'S PARISH CHURCH LANDSCAPE

The St. Paul's Parish Church site is located in the very northeastern portion of the College of Charleston's Stono River Preserve, formerly called Dixie Plantation (Figure 1.1). Here in an approximately 22.86 × 24.38 m (75 × 80 ft) clearing in the woods, about 45.72 m west of the Stono River and its marshes, is the only aboveground, visible evidence of St. Paul's original church—its cemetery. Four gravestones date to the period St. Paul's Parish Church was in use. In the northeastern portion of the clearing is a low mound, while a smaller, less obvious mound lies just to its south. Through ground-penetrating radar (GPR) and archaeological testing within St. Paul's church yard, it has been confirmed that the two slight mounds are the remains of the church (Pyszka et al. 2010). Of importance to this discussion are the results from GPR testing, collected and analyzed by Scott Harris from the College of Charleston. The GPR results clearly indicate that the mounds represent the ruins of a cruciform-shaped structure (Figure 1.2). The results also provide enough information to determine which mound represents the original 1707 church and which one was the addition. The two distinct construction phases of the church are clearly indicated—one a rectangle and the other forming the top portion of the cross. The rectangular portion of the church, later the "bottom" of the cross, measured 10.6 × 7.8 m (34.8 × 25.6 ft) from outside wall to outside wall. This is basically identical to the description provided by the vestrymen of St. Paul's Parish in 1715 of 10.67 × 7.62 m (35 × 25 ft). Thus, the original, rectangular church is represented by the small, less noticeable mound seen today, while the larger mound is the church addition.

The GPR results also show that the original rectangular church was situated on the landscape so that it was oriented northeast-southwest, with the congregation facing the northeast (Pyszka et al. 2010). This orientation

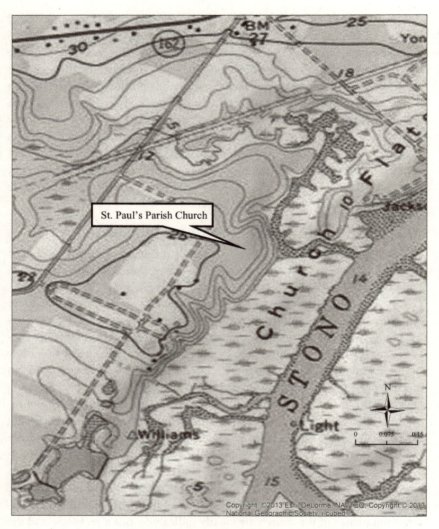

FIGURE 1.1. Detail of US Geological Survey Wadmalaw quadrangle map (updated 2012) indicating location of St. Paul's Parish Church ruins within the College of Charleston's Stono River Preserve. (Modified from base map copyright © 2013 Esri DeLorme, NAVTEQ, copyright © 2013 National Geographic Society, i-cubed; Kimberly Pyszka.)

FIGURE 1.2. Ground-penetrating radar (GPR)–generated image of St. Paul's churchyard. The 1707 church is represented by the rectangular portion of the footprint. The 1720s addition transformed the structure into a cruciform. The 1995 burial of John Henry Dick, who bequeathed the property to the College of Charleston, is seen within the original church's footprint. The root system of a live oak tree is also prominent. Image is taken at a depth of 50 cm and a 10 ns timeslice. (Image by Scott Harris. Reprinted from Kimberly Pyszka, Maureen Hays, and Scott Harris, "The Archaeology of St. Paul's Parish Church, Hollywood, SC, USA," *Church Archaeology* 12 [2010]: 73–80, Figure 3, with permission from Scott Harris and the Society for Church Archaeology.)

is unusual because Church of England canon law at the time stated that churches were to be oriented with the congregation facing east toward the altar and the rising sun. The east-facing orientation, important in Jewish synagogue construction, was adopted by the Catholic Church and later by the Church of England. The significance of the east can be seen in several biblical references, including Ezekiel 43:2, which reads, "and I saw the glory of the God of Israel coming from the east," and in Matthew 24:27, "just as lightning comes from the east and is seen as far as the west, so will the coming of the Son of Man be."

A study by Ali and Cunich (2005) of Anglican churches built in London between 1711 and 1734 indicated that all of them were placed on an east-west orientation. Most of the churches faced within three degrees of due east, while none were more than five degrees off the ideal alignment (2005:66). Their study shows that during this period, which corresponds to the time period when St. Paul's Parish Church and many others of the earliest Anglican churches in South Carolina were constructed, that architects and church designers still considered it important to orient churches to the east. The orientation of St. Paul's original church is approximately thirty-five degrees north of due east. Magnetic declination likely accounts for some of the offset, but the estimated declination in the Charleston area from 1750 to 2012 is only 8 percent (NOAA 2012). Magnetic declination also does not appear to be an issue in the offset seen at St. Paul's as many of the other churches in the region were oriented east-to-west, as expected.

If the church supervisors had placed their church on the traditional east-to-west orientation, the short axis of the building would have primarily been facing the river. By shifting the orientation the way they did, the long axis of the church sat directly parallel to the Stono River, the major waterway leading to the southern Indian lands. Their decision made the church a prominent feature on the landscape, projecting the presence of St. Paul's Church and the Anglican Church to all who traveled by. This alteration of the church's orientation to parallel a nearby waterway is similar to church construction practices presented in Lenik's (2010) research on Dominica. Could St. Paul's church supervisors have done the same thing for similar reasons? How and why did church supervisors decide on the specific location on which to build St. Paul's Church? What features of the landscape made this location attractive to them? Was St. Paul's oriented so that it faced the river a conscious decision? If so, was it a "materialization of ideology" as described by DeMarrais et al. (1996)?

Generally, the early Anglican churches in South Carolina were located as close to the center of the parish as possible and more importantly, along waterways. Another factor in church placement was high ground. In their 1980 study of settlement along the Stono River, South and Hartley showed that similar to the Jamestown, Santa Elena, and original Charles Towne settlements, late-seventeenth-century South Carolinians constructed their houses on high ground (at least 1.52 m (5 ft) above mean high water) along deep water (at least 0.91 m (3 ft). of water of mean low water) (South and Hartley 1980:24). Their "deep water and high ground" model should also apply to churches and other public buildings as they would have also needed to be on high enough ground to avoid problems with flooding during high tides yet have easy access to deep water. Hartley (1984) conducted a similar study along the nearby Ashley River with similar conclusions. The property donated by Landgrave Bellinger fit these desired characteristics as it was located along the Stono River, on high ground, and near the center of St. Paul's Parish. While their model initially appears to fit, it does not fully explain why church supervisors decided to place St. Paul's Church where they did. It is suggested here that there were other, more symbolic reasons for the placement of the church. Despite the fact that the church was located on high ground and near deep water, it sat in a relatively nonaccessible area and, therefore, deviates in part from South and Hartley's model. Currently, there are nearly 185 m of marsh separating the mainland from the river. At today's high tide, it would be impossible to get a boat up to the mainland.

Approximately 115 m to the north of the church site is a location that would have made an ideal boat landing area for St. Paul's parishioners arriving by boat. Here a tidal creek comes in from the Stono River and runs along a high bluff (1.5–3 m above water, depending on the tide). A plat from 1806 does label this area as a landing, but there is no indication if the landing dates back to the first half of the eighteenth century when services were held at the church (McCrady Plat No. 6611A 1806, Charleston County Register Mesne Conveyance Office, Charleston, South Carolina). Sixteen shovel tests of the area produced few historic artifacts (n=14). Most of the artifacts clearly dated to the nineteenth century, while only three delftware sherds could have dated to the early half of the eighteenth century. This testing suggests that the landing area was not used by St. Paul's parishioners to any great extent, if at all. This area of land, included in Bellinger's donation, would have made an ideal landing area for parishioners traveling by boat. Additionally, its location immediately along a deep-water creek with plenty of high, flat ground on which to build the church fits into South and Hartley's model.

It is suggested here that church supervisors consciously decided not to place St. Paul's Parish Church on this particular piece of high ground, which included deep water access, because along the tidal creek the church would not have made as much of a presence on the developing colonial landscape as it did along the Stono River. If they did decide to place St. Paul's Church in a more visible location, can the same be said for their decision to alter the orientation their church? In order to address this question and whether church landscape decisions fit DeMarrais et al.'s "materialization of ideology," it is necessary to move beyond St. Paul's Parish Church and examine the location and orientation of the other early-eighteenth-century Anglican churches in South Carolina. Through a regional approach, it will be possible to see whether any patterns in the placement of early-eighteenth-century Anglican churches on the South Carolina landscape emerge and possibly infer some reasoning behind their locations.

REGIONAL ANALYSIS OF ANGLICAN CHURCH ORIENTATION

The Church Act of 1706 called for the construction of churches in six parishes—Christ Church, St. Thomas', St. John's (Berkeley), St. James's (Goose Creek), St. Andrew's, and St. Paul's (Cooper 1837:237). Over the next decade, all nine parishes named in the 1706 Church Act had churches completed or under construction, with the exception of St. Bartholomew's. Through a combination of means, including archaeology, historical maps, site visits, and viewing extant structures on Google Earth, an attempt was made to locate the twelve Anglican churches and chapels constructed between 1706 and 1725. The only church that the location could not be identified was the one for St. James's (Santee) Parish, as the only description of its location is that it was along Echaw Creek, a tributary off the Santee River. Because its exact location could not be identified, the St. James's (Santee) church was eliminated from this study. The present-day churches of St. Thomas'/St. Denis', St. John's (Berkeley), and Christ Church are supposedly built on the locations of earlier churches. However, without archaeological or documentary evidence to substantiate those claims, those churches were also eliminated, leaving eight of the twelve churches and chapels constructed between 1706 and 1725 available for this study (Table 1.1). The elevation of the church or chapel above the waterway was determined using USGS topographic maps. Based on the locations of late-eighteenth to mid-eighteenth-century archaeological sites, including those identified by South and Hartley (1980), and standing structures, there does not appear to have been any significant changes in the topography of the region due to land use or environmental change in the past 300 years.

TABLE 1.1. South Carolina Anglican Churches and Chapels Constructed prior to 1725

Church or Chapel	Date	Building Material	Dimensions m (ft)	How Identified	Waterway	Elevation above Waterway m (ft)[a]	Location of Chancel
Parish Churches							
St. Andrew's	1706	brick	7.62 × 12.19 (25 × 40)	extant	Ashley River	3.0 (10)	southeast
St. Paul's	1707	brick	7.62 × 10.67 (25 × 35)	archaeology	Stono River	4.6 (15)	northeast
St. James's (Goose Creek)	1719	brick	10.67 × 13.7 (35 × 45)	extant	Goose Creek	6.1 (20)	east
St. George's	1719	brick	9.14 × 15.24 (30 × 50)	ruins	Ashley River	6.1 (20)	northeast
St. Philip's	1723	brick	18.3 × 24.38 (60 × 80)	historical document	n/a	n/a	east
St. Helena's	1724	brick	9.14 × 12.19 (30 × 40)	extant	Beaufort River	4.6 (15)	east
Parish Chapels of Ease							
St. James's (Goose Creek)	1724	brick	12.19 × 18.3 (40 × 60)	archaeology	n/a	n/a	east
St. John's (Berkeley) (Strawberry Chapel)	1724	brick	12.19 × 13.7 (40 × 45)	extant	Cooper River	6.1 (20)	east

[a]Elevations determined from USGS topographic maps.

A few patterns emerge while analyzing the specific landscape settings and the orientations of these eight buildings, with no apparent differences between the parish churches and their chapels of ease. Six of the structures were located on high ground (as defined by South and Hartley) immediately along a waterway. The placement of churches along waterways during the early decades of the colony is not surprising and does fit the deep water and high ground model. The use of waterways as roads made transportation easier even though some parishioners had to travel several miles to their place of worship. The General Assembly obviously recognized the importance of having the new Anglican churches located along major waterways. They wrote in the Church Act, "And whereas, it is necessary that six churches should be built for the publick worship of God, according to the Church of England; that is to say, one upon the South-east of Wandoe river, one upon that neck of land lying on the North-west of Wandoe, and South of Cooper river, one upon the Western branch of Cooper river, one upon Goose creek, one upon Ashley river, and one on the South side of Stono river in Colleton county" (Cooper 1837:283).

Of the six churches and chapels located along waterways, three of them—St. Paul's, St. Andrew's, and St. George's—deviated from the traditional east-to-west orientation as dictated by Church of England canon law, while the other three—St. James's (Goose Creek), St. Helena's, and Strawberry Chapel are oriented east-to-west. With the three churches that deviate in their expected orientation, the altering of the orientation led to the long axis of each church sitting parallel to the nearby waterway, leading to the churches being very prominent features on the landscape. St. Helena's Parish Church and Strawberry Chapel are situated on an east-to-west orientation that also places their long axes parallel to the Beaufort and Cooper Rivers, respectively. At this time it is not possible to state whether it is a coincidence that the east-west pattern placed them parallel to the rivers or if those lots were specifically chosen because that would satisfy both the traditional church orientation and the desire of church supervisors to have their church or chapel stand out to those traveling by on the water.

The only church along a waterway with its short axis facing the waterway is St. James's (Goose Creek). Unlike the Ashley, Stono, Cooper, and Beaufort Rivers which were major waterways used for trade and transportation, Goose Creek was a relatively minor waterway. It is a tidal creek off the Cooper River and the church is located approximately twelve miles upstream from their confluence. Today, Goose Creek ends about one mile upstream from the church and it becomes narrower and shallower, especially during low tides. Perhaps church supervisors at St. James's (Goose Creek) retained its east-to-west orientation because while people traveled *to* the church, few would have been traveling *by* the church.

Although the number of available churches and chapels available for this study is small, the results indicate that most of the early-eighteenth-century Anglican churches and chapels of ease were situated on the landscape in order to be as visible as possible from the nearby waterway. Unfortunately, there are few other buildings, extant or those studied archaeologically, to compare with the Anglican churches. A limited number of early-eighteenth-century domestic sites have been studied archaeologically and they indicate that planter houses were most likely to have their long axis face toward the south, allowing residents to advantage of sunlight during the winter months and the summer's cooling breezes; however, there is also some indication that planters also preferred to have their houses facing their fields and the nearest waterway (Poplin and Huddleston 1998:117–118). Due to the small amount of data available on non-Anglican buildings, this discussion will focus only on the Anglican structures.

The obvious question here is why would Anglican Church supervisors feel the need to make their religious buildings more visible? To answer this question, DeMarrais et al.'s "materialization of ideology" is applied. To do so, it is important to question the reasons why Anglican Church leaders felt the need to claim the land, to unify Anglicans, and to visually manifest their power.

Answers to these questions lay in the colony's political and religious conflicts during the early colonial period. During the opening decades of the eighteenth century, the rural parishes outside Charles Towne were in a tenuous position as they buffered the urban center from frontier lands still contested by the English, French, and Spanish, as well as various Native American groups. Because the Stono, Ashley, Cooper, and Beaufort Rivers were the primary transportation routes around the colony and into Indian lands, white settlers and traders would travel by the churches on a regular basis, likely on boats guided by enslaved Africans. Additionally, Native Americans still frequently used the waterways, especially in the southern parishes of St. Paul's, St. Bartholomew's, and St. Helena's. While several groups placed claim on the land, the placement of Anglican churches throughout the frontier made a statement to all other groups.

Another threat to the Anglican claim of the land came from the number of Dissenters living in the colony. Although there are no exact census figures regarding the numbers of Anglicans and Dissenters in the colony, it is estimated that in of the 4,000 white settlers living in South Carolina in 1700, 1,700 professed to be Anglican (Bolton 1982:19). In St. Paul's Parish Dissenters comprised a larger percentage of the parish population. In 1708,

St. Paul's Reverend Dun reported that of the "300 souls" living in the parish, "about 80 profess themselves Church of England" and "220 are dissenters" (Dun to SPG Secretary, September 20, 1708, SPG Microfilm Series A, Volume XIII:235–236). Many Dissenters also held powerful political positions in the General Assembly and sometimes even served as the colony's governor. The process of establishment had not been easy taking several years of debate and "tricky" politics. The majority of Dissenters in the colony and their increasing presence in colonial politics were additional reasons why Anglican Church supervisors felt a need to claim the land. They would have wanted to make it clear that they had "won" the battle over religious control of the colony and that the Church of England was there to stay. By placing rural Anglican churches in prominent positions along the waterways, the Church used the natural landscape and their churches to show their presence and communicate their power to all those who passed by—white and non-white, freed and enslaved, Anglicans and Dissenters.

Ultimately, South Carolina's early Anglican leaders deliberately created a cultural landscape that highlighted the presence and power of the Church of England. *Anglican churches were meant to be seen.* It was not just the Church that benefited from this purposeful display of Anglican influence and control. Especially in frontier parishes, such as St. Paul's, the Anglican churches also materially expressed the English "planting their flag" on Carolina soil, claiming it as their own over the rival claims of Indigenous groups, the French, and the Spanish.

ARCHITECTURE OF ST. PAUL'S PARISH CHURCH

While the specific placement of Anglican churches on the early colonial Carolina landscape conveyed messages, parish leaders also used architecture to communicate messages through the specific church design. Using evidence gained from archaeological excavations, historical documents, and extant churches, in this section I explore the design and overall architectural style of St. Paul's Parish Church. As with their use of the landscape, parish leaders designed their church to express their goals and represent the religiously diverse makeup of white settlers in their parish.

While the GPR testing and data provided information on the overall positioning and layout of St. Paul's Parish Church, archaeological excavations supplied the necessary evidence to learn about the construction materials used and details of specific interior features. Excavations at the site began in 2009 and continued over the next two years. In total, crew members, comprised mainly of College of Charleston students, excavated a dozen 1.52 m² (5 ft²) test units and a single 0.3 × 2.13 m (1 × 7 ft) trench within the structure's footprint (Figure 1.3). Relying on the GPR data and architectural information from extant eighteenth-century Anglican churches, excavation units were placed in strategic locations to glean the most information about the church's overall plan, such as the location of entrances, aisles, and the chancel. This method proved to be very successful, as excavations revealed a number of architectural features about the original, rectangular 1707 church, as well as its 1720s addition. Despite the absence of visual documentation of St. Paul's, this combination of data has led to a better understanding of its overall visual appearance.

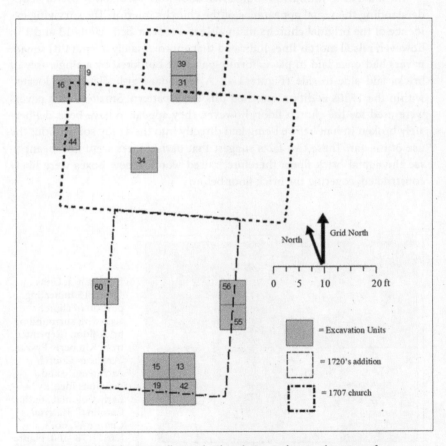

FIGURE 1.3. Map of the St. Paul's Parish Church site, indicating location of excavations within church footprint. (Reprinted from Kimberly Pyszka, "Anglican Church Architecture and Religious Identity in Early Colonial South Carolina," *Material Culture* 49, no. 1 [2017]: 78–100, Figure 4, with permission from the International Society for Landscape, Place, and Material Culture.)

Archaeological excavations revealed several architectural features, including several sections of the foundation, portions of the church's aisles and brick floor, location of entrances, and an architectural separation between the nave and the chancel of the post-1720s church. The foundation width, 0.55 m (1.8 ft), was the same for both the original church and its addition. Tim Riordan's study of Virginia churches indicates a strong correlation between the foundation's width and the height of the structure. Based on his research, a 0.55 m (1.8 ft) wide foundation suggests approximately 3.96 m (13 ft) high walls, or a one-story building (Hurry 2011).

The main aisle and surrounding brick floor were particularly useful in understanding the visual appearance of the church's interior. The surviving evidence of the original church's main aisle is a mortar bed (Units 13 and 15); however, raised mortar lines indicated that approximately 0.3 m (1 ft) square pavers had once laid in place, forming an aisle bordered by a single row of bricks laid side-to-side (Figure 1.4). A secondary aisle (Unit 34) located within the 1720s addition matched this same pattern. Smaller brick pavers were used for the church floor; however, they appear to have been deliberately broken in half before being laid directly into the sandy soil without the use of mortar. These two facts suggest that parishioners were not meant to see the actual brick floor; therefore, raised wooden pew boxes were likely constructed, covering the brick floor below.

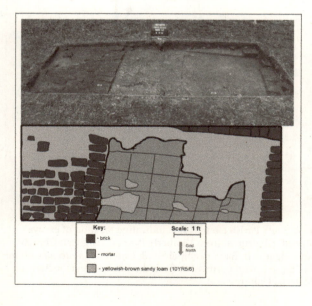

FIGURE 1.4. Units 13 and 15 indicating portion of church aisle with surrounding brick floor. (Reprinted from Kimberly Pyszka, "Anglican Church Architecture and Religious Identity in Early Colonial South Carolina," *Material Culture* 49, no. 1 [2017]: 78–100, Figure 5, with permission from the International Society for Landscape, Place, and Material Culture.)

Based on extant eighteenth-century rectangular Anglican churches, the original St. Paul's likely had either two or three entrances—one centered along the west side and one centered on the north and possibly, south walls. Excavations centered on the west wall revealed the church's main entrance as evidenced by an intact 1.52 m (5 ft) wide brick threshold (Units 19 and 42). Archaeologists also identified the disturbed remains of a brick threshold centered along the church's south wall (Units 55 and 56). This entrance was only 0.91 m (3 ft) wide, likely a secondary entrance into the 1707 church. Although excavations at this location were not continued into the church's interior, a secondary aisle must have led parishioners to the main aisle. Unfortunately, excavations along St. Paul's north wall were inconclusive as to whether an entrance had been located there or not (Unit 60).

Once the church was transformed into a cruciform, the south entrance (and north if one was present) would have no longer been desired and, therefore, was closed off, likely accounting for its disturbed nature. Instead, two entrances would have been located in the newly constructed addition at the end of each transept of the "cross." An entrance with a single step that led parishioners into the church was uncovered along the north transept (Unit 44). Unfortunately, the presence of large trees in the immediate vicinity of the likely south transept entrance impeded excavations at that location.

Many colonial Anglican churches had an architectural separation of some sort that separated the nave from the more sacred chancel, and St. Paul's was no different. Due to the presence of the 1995 grave of the property owner at the time, excavations in the location of the original 1707 church's chancel have not been conducted. However, within the church's addition at the far end of the church aisle a single step leads into the chancel (Unit 31). Strawberry Chapel has a similar step; however, its "step" is actually the place where communicants kneeled during communion. The "step" at St. Paul's likely served the same purpose.

Architectural debris including brick, glazed brick, mortar, plaster, colorless window glass, and wrought nails comprised a vast majority of the artifact assemblage. While such artifacts are not that helpful in learning more about parishioner activities, they do allow for interpretations about the overall appearance of St. Paul's Parish Church.

Among the numerous brick fragments recovered, a few showed evidence of glazing. Glazed bricks were typically not glazed on purpose, but instead were those bricks exposed to the greatest amount of heat during the firing process (McKee 1973:44). Such bricks often highlight the corners, windows, and doorways of buildings. Crew members found glazed brick fragments in nearly every excavation unit, but not in enough quantity to indicate where or how they were used. Recovered artifacts also included several fragments of white-painted plaster that once covered interior walls. There is no evidence the church's exterior walls had been covered in stucco. Recovered window glass fragments were colorless, or discolored naturally over time, with no evidence of stained glass. Forty small roofing nails (less than 3 cm) suggest the church had a wood-shingled roof, an idea further supported by the absence of slate or clay roofing tiles.

In addition to verifying the location of the ruins of St. Paul's Parish Church, archaeological investigations led to many previously unknown discoveries about its visual appearance. Due to the subsurface ruins of St. Paul's, there are some limitations on what can be determined regarding its visual appearance. However, by combining the information obtained through excavations, GPR survey, historic documents, and the architecture of extant churches, it is now possible to at least partially visualize St. Paul's Parish Church, well beyond its sole surviving description as "a Small but convenient Brick Church in length 35 in breadth 25 feet" (10.67 × 7.62 m) (St. Paul's

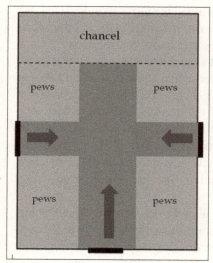

FIGURE 1.5. Conceptual layout of original 1707 St. Paul's Parish Church. (Reprinted from Kimberly Pyszka, "Anglican Church Architecture and Religious Identity in Early Colonial South Carolina," *Material Culture* 49, no. 1 [2017]: 78–100, Figure 6, with permission from the International Society for Landscape, Place, and Material Culture.)

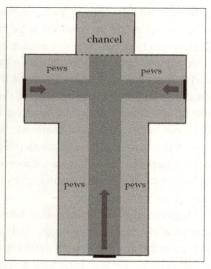

FIGURE 1.6. Conceptual layout of post-1720s St. Paul's Parish Church. (Reprinted from Kimberly Pyszka, "Anglican Church Architecture and Religious Identity in Early Colonial South Carolina," *Material Culture* 49, no. 1 [2017]: 78–100, Figure 7, with permission from the International Society for Landscape, Place, and Material Culture.)

Parish Vestry to SPG Secretary, January 20, 1715, SPG Microfilm Series B, Volume IV:41).

The one-story-tall brick church likely had decorative glazed bricks accenting its corners, windows, and/or doorways and was covered with a wood-shingled roof. From 1707 to the 1720s, entrances along the west and south sides of the church, and possibly its north side, welcomed parishioners for church services (Figure 1.5). As they entered the church, the white-plastered interior walls and the natural light coming through the colorless, glazed windows would have made the church interior very bright and welcoming, while the barrel-vaulted ceiling, similar to those at the region's other Anglican churches, gave the church a very open feel. A 2.13 m (7 ft)-wide center aisle ran the long axis of the church, ending at the chancel, while a secondary aisle led parishioners from the south entrance to the center aisle. During services, parishioners sat in raised wooden pew boxes located on either side of the aisle, facing the pulpit and the chancel where wooden tablets likely hung on the walls depicting the Lord's Prayer and Ten Commandments.

With the completion of the addition in 1732, the south entrance (and north entrance if present) into the original section of the church was closed off (Figure 1.6). The center aisle now extended to the new chancel, which was separated from the nave by a step and wooden railing where communicants knelt. An additional aisle intersected the main aisle just before the chancel, leading to two new entrances at the end of each transept. With the completion of wooden pew boxes in the addition, St. Paul's Parish Church now held approximately 200 parishioners (Bull to SPG Secretary, October 10, 1722, SPG Microfilm Series B, Volume IV:240–241). For the next twenty years or so, services continued at the newly expanded church without any further renovations or remodeling.

ST. PAUL'S ARCHITECTURE AS EXPRESSION OF RELIGIOUS AND SOCIAL IDEOLOGY

More than just providing a visual picture of St. Paul's Parish Church, this study also allows for discussion on how it represented the religious ideology of the South Carolina Anglican Church, its leaders, and residents of St. Paul's Parish. As seen in pre-Reformation England, elaborately decorated Catholic churches with their wall paintings and iconography changed greatly as a result of the Reformation. As Protestantism replaced Catholicism, church interiors became more sparsely furnished and lacked décor due to Puritan ideas of simplicity and practicality. As large numbers of Puritans left England for the New World, their teachings continued to influence the Church of England, especially its colonial churches.

Changes in church doctrine did not end with the Reformation. At the time the Carolina colony was planned and organized, some Catholic influences had returned to the Church. Elaborate clergy vestments, making the sign of the cross, and a return to the importance of communion became standard again (Rosman 2003:105). Many English churches saw a return to the grand and elaborate styles as seen in Christopher Wren's late seventeenth-century London churches, even though Wren designed his churches so that the focus was on the Puritan idea of hearing the sermon (Nelson 2008:22–23; Upton 1986:56–67). This combination of Puritan and Catholic influences led to a growing division within the Church between High churchmen and Low churchmen. High churchmen believed in a strict following of Anglican teachings and at least a greater alliance, if not a return, to the Catholic Church (Doran and Durston 2003:91). In contrast, Low churchmen believed in the Puritan way of life and were more open to religious tolerance. In the Americas, especially the American colonies, Low Church beliefs dominated; however, High Church followers were also influential.

When South Carolina's General Assembly established the Church of England and Anglican parish leaders designed their churches, this division was still an issue (Bolton 1971, 1982). That division is a possible reason for the two distinct architectural styles seen among South Carolina's eighteenth-century Anglican churches. Based on the three extant structures and drawings of the original St. Philip's Church, which no longer exists, the exterior appearance of many churches, especially the rural ones, were rather plain. Interior walls lacked decorations, with the only exception being wooden tablets that hung on the chancel walls that depicted the Lord's Prayer and Ten Commandments. Interior furnishings were also rather simple, with plain wooden pews or raised wooden pew boxes, a pulpit, an altar table, and a baptismal font. Of South Carolina's surviving Anglican churches, today's St. Andrew's and Strawberry Chapel (Figure 1.7) are examples of the plain churches, which for lack of a better term will be referred to as "Low" churches.

Undoubtedly, there have been some renovations to both churches over time. Stucco now covers the brick exterior walls of both buildings, while roofs and windows have been replaced as needed. Reverend Guy's 1728 account of St. Andrew's describes the overall church layout much as it appears today, including the placement of doorways and windows. He also described fairly plain and simple interior features—"neat Cedar pews," "a decent font," and "well glazd" windows (Guy to SPG Secretary, January 22, 1728, SPG Microfilm Series A, Volume XX:110–115). Similarly, there is little evidence to suggest that Strawberry Chapel's interior appeared significantly different from how it does today, with the exception that its original pulpit was

FIGURE 1.7. Exterior and interior of Strawberry Chapel. (Reprinted from Kimberly Pyszka, "Anglican Church Architecture and Religious Identity in Early Colonial South Carolina," *Material Culture* 49, no. 1 [2017]: 78–100, Figures 8 and 9, with permission from the International Society for Landscape, Place, and Material Culture.)

removed (Linder 2000). Aside from the addition of the stucco, Strawberry Chapel's simple exterior has changed little and is considered the best representation of most of the colony's rural Anglican pre-1740 churches (Nelson 2008:299).

Figure 1.8. Exterior and interior of St. James's (Goose Creek) Church, 2012. (Photographs by Jeremy C. Miller. Reprinted from Kimberly Pyszka, "Anglican Church Architecture and Religious Identity in Early Colonial South Carolina," *Material Culture* 49, no. 1 [2017]: 78–100, Figures 10 and 11, with permission from Jeremy C. Miller and the International Society for Landscape, Place, and Material Culture.)

In contrast, St. James's (Goose Creek) (Figure 1.8) is an example of a "High" church with its ornate interior features including molded plaster cherubs and flaming hearts over arched doorways, interior memorials, and elaborate chancel walls. While the church has seen its share of renovations and repairs over the past 300 years, it appears that the church has always been elaborate. In 1727, Reverend Ludlam described some of its interior features as, "two rows of round timber pillars, painted marble [illegible], together with an altar piece decently beautified with paintgs & guildings grave & commendable" (Ludlam to SPG Secretary, December 12, 1727, SPG Microfilm Series A, Volume XX:98-104). It is also believed that the interior woodwork is original (National Register of Historic Places 1976). Additionally, the dates engraved on interior memorials and small-scale archaeological studies indicate that many interior features are either original, original but moved, or replaced to appear original (Linder 2000:24; Nelson 2009:73). The exterior is equally ornate with its baroque features including pilasters around the doorways and decorative masonry work detail, which are seen in Charles Fraser's ca. 1800 watercolor of the church. Despite some changes, St. James's (Goose Creek) likely appears similar to as it did when construction was completed ca. 1719.

St. James's (Goose Creek) High Church characteristics are not overly surprising considering the makeup of the parish's population. Among the parish's residents were the "Goose Creek Men," an influential group of wealthy planters. Before settling in Carolina, they had already established themselves on Barbados, where along with Jamaica, High Church influences prevailed (Nelson 2009). Described as a "party of fervent Anglicans" (Nelson 2008:253), the Goose Creek Men were powerful political players who were instrumental in the establishment of the Anglican Church. Additionally, Reverend Francis Le Lau, the SPG missionary assigned to St. James's (Goose Creek), allied himself with the High Church and did not hide his dislike of dissenting groups (Bolton 1971:67-68). His leanings likely also factored into the overall design of their church.

In the same aforementioned 1727 letter, Ludlam wrote that in comparison to the other churches in the colony, St. James's (Goose Creek) "excell in Beauty, all other Churches at present in the Province except St. Philips, in Charles Town" (Ludlam to SPG Secretary, December 12, 1727, SPG Microfilm Series A, Volume XX:98-104). The early eighteenth-century St. Philip's Church only survives through drawings and description; however, it would also be categorized as a High church based on its grandeur and lavish architectural details and interior furnishings. St. Philip's exterior had features uncommon in colonial churches, such as porticos, pilasters, and a cupola with bells and a clock. Multiple aisles, arches, columns, pilasters, and cornices graced the large, two-story, open nave. St. Philip's expressed more of the High Church ideals that had gained strength in England during late-seventeenth and early eighteenth centuries. Additionally, St. Philip's elaborate design may have been meant to express more than High Church influences. Nelson (2008:38) attributes its ornate design to Charles Town's wealthy Anglican businessmen who wished to express to the world that their city was not an isolated frontier town.

Based on the overall floor plan, size, and construction materials, St. Paul's likely appeared very similar to Strawberry Chapel and therefore, was a "Low" church. Written documents also provide evidence that St. Paul's residents were more likely to have followed Low Church practices and ideas. From its 1706 founding, the parish was known for its large number of Dissenters. In 1708, St. Paul's Reverend William Dun provided the SPG with a parish census, reporting that the population included approximately 300 individuals with eighty "professing themselves as belonging to the Church of England." He further noted that the parish's 220 Dissenters consisted of 150 Presbyterians, 8 Independents, 40 Anabaptists, 10 Quakers, "& above 12 others, whom I cannot tell what to make of" (Dun to SPG Secretary, September 20, 1708, SPG Microfilm Series A, Volume XIII:235–236). Presbyterians, who comprised a majority of the parish's population, were well known for some of the most stringent Puritan practices.

Each individual parish's church supervisors were charged with all decisions regarding the construction of its church. For St. Paul's, that task fell to Seabrook, Hicks, and Farr. While we will never know their motivations behind the church's design, it is believed they intentionally designed St. Paul's as a "Low" church to represent the parish's religious diversity. They recognized that a majority of parish residents were Dissenters, specifically Presbyterians. By following a more Puritan-influenced architectural design for St. Paul's, they may have consciously appealed to the large number of Dissenters living in the parish and who would hopefully attend church services. Therefore, by designing an Anglican church that appealed to Dissenters, St. Paul's church supervisors expressed the underlying ideology of South Carolina since its initial founding—that it was a religiously tolerant colony that accepted people of many faiths.

In examining other parishes and their churches, a similar pattern is seen. In St. Andrew's Parish, Dissenters also made up a majority of the population (Guy to SPG Secretary, July 5, 1721, SPG Microfilm Series A, Volume XV:50–51; Taylor to SPG Secretary, July 28, 1713, SPG Microfilm Series A, Volume 8, Letter 14). St. John's Parish's Strawberry Chapel also appears to be a

"Low" church. While in its early years, St. John's Parish had a majority of Anglicans (Maule to SPG Secretary, 1710, SPG Microfilm Series A, Volume III, Letter CXXXIII), by the late 1710s and early 1720s, letters indicate the parish had difficulties in finding and keeping a minister, which may have led to an increase in the dissenter population by the time Strawberry Chapel was built (Bull to SPG Secretary, May 12, 1719, SPG Microfilm Series B, Volume IV:40–42; Churchwardens and Vestrymen of St. John's Parish to General Nicholson, February 6, 1722, SPG Microfilm Series A, Volume XVI:54). Meanwhile, Anglicans comprised a vast majority of the white population in the High Church parishes of St. James's (Goose Creek) and St. Philip's (Le Jau to SPG Secretary, December 2, 1706, SPG Microfilm Series A, Volume III, Letter 78; Thomas 1905:31–32). Not only did Anglicans comprise a majority, but they were also some of the most powerful political officials, such as the Goose Creek Men.

Another consideration for the more elaborate churches in St. James's (Goose Creek) and St. Philip's Parishes is the overall wealth of parishioners. These two parishes had their share of wealthy, powerful men, and so did St. Andrew's and St. Paul's. Landgrave Edmund Bellinger, one of the largest landholders in the colony and a powerful government official, Joseph Blake, a two-term governor, and several members of the General Assembly all lived within St. Paul's Parish, while St. Andrew's Parish was the home of several of the richest men in the colony, including the Drayton, Middleton, and Bull families. In 1728, SPG missionary Brian Hunt specifically referred to these four rural parishes—St. Paul's, St. Andrew's, St. James's (Goose Creek), and St. John's—as the "wealthy" parishes (Hunt to SPG Secretary, October 5, 1728, SPG Microfilm Series A, Volume XXI:127–130). While the possibilities that St. James's (Goose Creek) and St. Philip's had more elaborate church architecture due to wealth cannot be ruled out, St. Paul's and St. Andrew's parishes also had their share of wealthy men, many who made their fortunes from the prime rice-producing lands in those parishes.

During its fifty-year existence, St. Paul's Parish Church left its mark on the parish landscape and its residents. Likewise, the Church of England influenced the development of the South Carolina colony and the religious and social lives of all people who lived there. Through their deliberate use of natural landscape features, namely the Stono River, parish leaders materially expressed the presence and power of the Anglican Church, as well as that of the English. Additionally, as seen at St. Paul's, they designed their church so that its visual appearance reflected the religiously diverse white population of the parish. By doing so, white settlers within St. Paul's formed a new community. As an unintended consequence of these trends, white settlers began to overlook the religious differences among themselves and began to identify themselves based on skin color rather than religious background. In chapter 4, I will explore this idea of community formation around a new Carolina, white identity. For now, however, our story turns to St. Luke's Episcopal Church in Cahaba, Alabama.

CHAPTER TWO

St. Luke's Episcopal Church, Cahaba, Alabama

> It will not be without a beneficial influence, situated as it is upon the banks of the Alabama, in sight of all the travel upon that thoroughfare; and many another church will unconsciously owe its grace and fair proportions to St. Luke's Church, Cahaba.
>
> —Reverend George F. Cushman, St. Luke's Episcopal Church (Cushman 1854:252)

IN DECEMBER 2019 Alabama celebrated the bicentennial of its statehood. Commemoration events were held throughout the state, most notably in Montgomery, the current state capital, and at Old Cahawba Archaeological Park, the location of Alabama's first capital and statehouse. Cahawba served as the state capital for only six years, but its best days were yet to come. After an initial decline when the capital moved to Tuscaloosa in 1826, the town's population rebounded, largely due to fertile soils ideal for cotton cultivation. Over three decades, Cahaba (now spelled without the "w") prospered economically and socially.[1] At the brink of the Civil War, several mansions, commercial businesses, hotels, theaters, schools, and churches dotted the Cahaba landscape. After the Civil War, Cahaba declined rapidly and since the 1930s has been a "ghost town." Today, the Alabama Historical Commission (AHC)

Figure 2.1. 1854 St. Luke's Episcopal Church in its current location at Old Cahawba Archaeological Park. (Photograph by Kimberly Pyszka.)

manages Old Cahawba Archaeological Park. Only a handful of features remain on the former town's landscape, including its streets, cemeteries, artisan wells, some structural ruins, and although moved from its original location, the 1854 St. Luke's Episcopal Church (Figure 2.1).

With the benefit of an extant structure available for study, in this chapter I place more emphasis on the religious and social meanings of St. Luke's architecture than I could in the case of St. Paul's. However, the landscape choices made by parish officials also held meaning and significance and are thus also considered. Although St. Luke's has been moved, evidence from archaeological excavations at its original location, an 1872 drawing of the church, and photographs and drawings from the 1936 Historic American Buildings Survey (HABS) indicates that beyond the removal of its bell tower (with the spire) and the removal of its gallery, the extant building has seen little alteration since its construction.

St. Luke's is a prime example of the Gothic Revival style of architecture. Characteristics of Gothic Revival include an emphasis on verticality, such as steeply pitched roofs, lancet windows and doorways, and more ornate and decorative features, including buttresses and decorative trim along the gable ends (McAlester and McAlester 2000:197–198). During the mid-nineteenth century, Gothic Revival was widely employed in a variety of structures. Importantly for the case under consideration, it was the architectural style of choice for the Episcopal Church, arising as it did largely as a response to ideological changes within it. Beginning in the early to mid-nineteenth century, both the Church of England and the Protestant Episcopal Church in the United States shifted away from the Low Church ideology of the eighteenth century, returning to High Church ideology and principles (Stanton 1997). More specifically, St. Luke's is an example of Carpenter Gothic architecture. A subcategory of Gothic Revival, Carpenter Gothic arose primarily in frontier and rural areas, such as Cahaba. While generally having the same characteristics as Gothic Revival architecture, Carpenter Gothic adapted to the skill level of local carpenters and to the available natural resources specific to a given region.

In this chapter, I discuss how St. Luke's Episcopal Church leaders used architecture as a materialization of the High Church ideology of the Episcopal Church and the Diocese of Alabama that proliferated in the mid-nineteenth century. They also used architecture, along with the local landscape, to communicate their identity, ideologies, wealth and status, and goals. Among the latter were to showcase Cahaba as a cosmopolitan, modern town and to uphold current social ideas regarding the segregation of Black people, whether enslaved or not.

CAHABA HISTORICAL OVERVIEW

American Indian populations, in particular ancestors of today's Muscogee (Creek) Nation and the Poarch Creek Band of Creek Indians, had occupied the lands of Alabama for centuries. However, Cahaba's Euro-American history begins in the late 1810s as the Alabama Territory prepared to become a state. William Wyatt Bibb, then-governor of the territory, was instrumental in the Alabama Territory General Assembly designating Cahawba as the state's first capital. Despite there being no existing town, or even a settlement, he argued the lands at the confluence of the Alabama and Cahaba Rivers were a suitable location for the capital, largely due to their location along the navigable Alabama River. Additionally, in his November 8, 1818, message to the General Assembly, Bibb wrote that this location was advantageous due to the "abundant production of an extensive and fertile back Country on the Alabama and Cahawba and their tributary streams the town of Cahawba promises to vie with the largest inland towns in the Country" (Brantley 1976:61). Another benefit of Bibb's proposed capital location was that it was centrally located within Alabama Territory, relatively close to the higher population density in its northern parts while still having direct river access to Mobile and its ports. More important to Bibb, the land had yet to be sold. He believed that money raised by the sale of lots would help with his efforts to build Alabama's treasury (Brantley 1976; Derry 2000; Roark 1985:267).

Bibb's campaign succeeded. In November 1818 the Alabama Territory General Assembly passed an act stating that "the Seat of Government shall be established permanently at the town of Cahawba" (Alabama Legislative Acts, 1818, Second Session, Alabama Department of Archives and History, Montgomery). Nevertheless, at the time Bibb's capital only existed on paper. In this still wilderness land, lots had to be surveyed and sold, roads cleared, and buildings constructed (Brantley 1976; Derry 2000). Cahawba grew quickly, with a number of structures completed by 1820, including residential and commercial buildings, schools, hotels, a theater, and, most importantly, the new temporary statehouse. Upon Bibb's death in 1820, Cahawba lost its most prominent and influential supporter. Within a few years, the Alabama legislature voted to move the state capital out of Cahawba to Tuscaloosa.[2]

With the relocation of the capital, Cahawba's population and status in the state waned rapidly. However, as already indicated, this decline was relatively short-lived. In 1829 the state gifted the former statehouse to Dallas County, and the town, now spelled Cahaba, became the county seat. This new honor led to the town's revival and substantial growth in its population, social influence, and economic prosperity. By the late 1850s, the population reached an estimated 3,000 to 6,000 citizens (Derry 2000:18). A key factor in Cahaba's antebellum success was the "fertile back Country" that Governor Bibb originally noted in 1818. The lands of Central Alabama's "Black Belt" were considered some of the best state lands for cotton production (Abernathy 1965:31). Additionally, Cahaba's direct river access to Mobile's ports along the Gulf of Mexico made it relatively easy for planters to transport and sell their cotton and other goods to the larger cities along the East Coast and throughout the entire Atlantic World.

The fertile lands and river access contributed significantly to Cahaba's "heyday." By the 1850s, Cahaba not only served as the county seat but was also home to a number of businesses, grand houses, restaurants, hotels, educational academies, churches (including St. Luke's Episcopal Church), a riverboat landing, and the railroad (Roark 1985; Scott 2011:18). Its residents included some of the wealthiest merchants and planters in the state and Dallas County was reportedly the fourth wealthiest county in the United States in the years leading up to the Civil War (Scott 2011:18). In addition to their free, affluent citizens, Cahaba and the surrounding area were also home to a number of people born into slavery. From the time of its founding in 1818, enslaved peoples provided the labor for Cahaba and the region's agriculture success. In 1818 enslaved peoples comprised 20 to 30 percent of Dallas County's overall population (Abernathy 1965:73). By 1830 the enslaved population had grown to over 50 percent, largely due to the development of new technologies that led to an increase in cotton production despite the challenging soils of the Black Belt (Abernathy 1965:74, 76). In the 1860 United States Census, 76.6 percent of the county's 33,625 reported individuals are listed as enslaved.

Cahaba's glory days peaked as the United States teetered on the verge of civil war. According to the 1860 United States Census, 1,920 people lived in the town of Cahaba itself—1,200 of whom were enslaved. As seen in many parts of the South, wartime casualties and subsequent destruction of the landscape led to severe economic and population declines. At the time of the 1870 United States Census, Cahaba's population had sharply declined to 431 individuals, of whom 302 were reported as "coloreds" (Scott 2011:20–21). In addition to the general effects of war, a series of specific events during the early 1860s also contributed to this steep falloff of the population. In 1862 Confederate troops dismantled the railroad between Selma and Demopolis, which ran through Cahaba, for the purpose of using the materials elsewhere (Scott 2011:19). As the war was coming to its end, a devastating flood reportedly covered the entire town in water. In 1866 Dallas County officials transferred the county seat from Cahaba to Selma, providing the proverbial "final nail in the coffin" to the once-prosperous town. These events, in conjunction with the loss of enslaved labor due to emancipation, led to the exodus of most of Cahaba's white population, with many people relocating to Selma. As they left, they dismantled many of their houses and commercial buildings to use the materials elsewhere. In some cases, they moved entire structures to Selma. Within a few years, Cahaba's commercial district all but ceased to exist (Roark 1985; Scott 2011).

From that point on, only a few white families remained among the remnants of the former state capital and once-prosperous river town. At the same time, many newly freed African Americans either stayed in Cahaba or moved there after living and laboring in the surrounding cotton fields of Dallas County. Despite the African American community that developed, Cahaba's population continued to decline. By 1880 it had dwindled to the point that Cahaba was not even recognized as a town for that year's census (Scott 2011:21). Although a few Black and white families continued to live within the former town boundaries, by the end of the 1930s only the streets and a few structures remained (Scott 2011).

Since 1975 the AHC has managed, protected, and interpreted Cahaba, now Old Cahawba Archaeological Park. The AHC, with assistance from the Cahaba Foundation (formed in 2008), has purchased parcel of lands in an attempt to regain as much of the original town layout as possible (Derry 2012:55). Even though only a handful of structures and other landscape features remain, Old Cahawba attracts visitors interested in learning about its history and its cultural and natural resources.

ST. LUKE'S EPISCOPAL CHURCH: PAST AND PRESENT

Despite St. Luke's Episcopal Church not being officially organized until 1839, as early as 1822 seven Episcopalian families lived and worshipped in Cahawba. Although they would not have a dedicated church building until over two decades later, members met monthly to read the Book of Prayer together. After the Alabama legislature moved the state capital out of Cahawba, the number of Episcopalians in the community declined, along with the population in general. However, by the late 1820s Cahaba had begun its revitalization and, thus, so did the Episcopalian congregation. Even though they were still without a church building, they met for services in the county courthouse (Caldwell 1997:1–2).

In addition to Episcopalians, Cahaba was the home of a number of other Christian denominations, including Methodists, Presbyterians, Baptists, and Cumberland Presbyterians. Especially in the early years of the town's development, congregations remained small, and their funds limited. Therefore, in 1840 these different organizations banded together and constructed the Union Church (occasionally referred to as the "Cahaba Church" or "Old Church"), with each group using the church building on a rotating schedule for their respective services (Fry 1905:127; Roark 1985:269). As Cahaba continued to grow and became the social and economic center of Dallas County, as well as much of Central Alabama, each of the individual church organizations eventually constructed their own dedicated church, leaving the Baptists to use the former Union Church building (Scott 2011:18).

After several years of meeting and worshipping together unofficially, in 1839 the Episcopalian Diocese of Alabama officially organized St. Luke's Parish (Protestant Episcopal Church, Diocese of Alabama 1839:7). As Cahaba continued to grow and prosper through the 1840s and into the 1850s, so did St. Luke's membership. However, they remained without a dedicated church building. In the late 1840s, the parish began to collect donations for a church building of their own. Similar to Episcopalian congregations elsewhere, some of the community's wealthiest families comprised St. Luke's congregation, including merchants and professionals living in town, as well as planters from the surrounding Dallas County area (Caldwell 1997:2–3).

For example, originally from Staten Island, Edward Perine was among Cahaba's earliest residents and had become a very successful merchant with his own store in the center of Cahaba. Perine was actively involved in leadership of the parish, serving as a vestryman, parish secretary, warden, and a convention delegate. He was also instrumental in the parish acquiring the funds to construct their church (Caldwell 1997:6).

At a meeting on April 8, 1853, St. Luke's vestrymen passed a motion that allowed for the construction to begin. Perine, along with St. Luke's Reverend Mitchell and Judge William Hunter, served on the building committee (St. Luke's Vestry Minutes, April 8, 1853, Old Cahawba Archaeological Park Archives). They hired David Cumming as the contractor, along with his assistant, Mr. Lipkin (Dallas Gazette, March 31, 1854). Construction on the church began in 1853, at an estimated cost of $5,000. When completed, St. Luke's exceeded its original budget with the final expenses totaling $6,000 (Cushman 1855:148; Protestant Episcopal Church, Diocese of Alabama 1853:11). On April 1, 1854, the first services were held (Figure 2.2). A few

FIGURE 2.2. Drawing of St. Luke's Episcopal Church, 1872, by A. M. Vasser, who grew up in Cahaba. (Courtesy of Alabama Department of Archives and History.)

weeks later, on May 14, Bishop Cobbs of the Diocese of Alabama consecrated the church (Protestant Episcopal Church, Diocese of Alabama 1854:12).

Just a few years later, the Civil War began, marking the end of Cahaba's zenith. As the town's population declined, in particular its white population, so did St. Luke's membership. By around 1870 congregation numbers had fallen so drastically that the parish dissolved, leaving the church vacant. At the request of a local Episcopalian congregation, in 1878 the former St. Luke's structure was moved to Martin's Station, approximately fifteen miles west of Cahaba. For the next twenty years or so, it served as a place of worship for a different Episcopalian congregation, until they abandoned it as well. The building once again served as a place of worship when, in the early 1900s, the property owner allowed a Black Baptist congregation to use the building for their worship services. Eventually renaming the edifice the Azion Baptist Church, this congregation worshipped in it for most of the twentieth century. Unfortunately, with limited funds for maintenance, the aging structure eventually fell into disrepair. In the early 2000s, the Cahawba Advisory Committee worked with the trustees of Azion Baptist Church and the AHC to return the building to Cahaba after raising funds for a new church building for the Azion Baptist congregation (Cahaba Advisory Committee 2017).

In 2007 Auburn University's Rural Studio program carefully documented and disassembled the structure, labeling each individual part. With the building completely dismantled, students and faculty moved the pieces to Old Cahawba Archaeological Park, where they reassembled St. Luke's piece by piece (Auburn University Rural Studio 2022a, 2022b). Due to flooding concerns at its original location at the intersection of Vine Street and First Street South, they reassembled the structure immediately across the road from the park's Visitor's Center. Despite its multiple relocations and complete disassembly, St. Luke's Episcopal Church visual appearance has changed little since it first opened for services in 1854.

The floorplan of St. Luke's approximates a 23.77 × 9.14 m (78 × 30 ft) cruciform. The exterior is covered in vertical board-and-batten siding, a hallmark feature of Carpenter Gothic structures. Other common features of Gothic Revival architecture are also apparent—namely, its emphasis on verticality and ornamental features. St. Luke's vertical appearance was highlighted in three ways—the use of vertical board-and-batten siding, the since-removed bell tower with a spire that once reached 27.43 m (90 ft) above the ground surface, and its tall, narrow lancet windows. In addition to emphasizing the structure's verticality, these latter also added to its ornateness. This was especially true of the triple lancet window feature that overlooks the chancel. Today, these windows are colorless glass; however, at the time of St. Luke's construction, they were stained glass. Removed in 1878, the original triplet of stained-glass windows is now located in the chancel of St. Andrew's Episcopal Church in Prairieville, approximately fifty miles west of Cahaba. Exterior buttresses along the nave walls add to the ornate feel of St. Luke's.

St. Luke's interior is divided into four distinct areas. The largest section is the roughly 17.68 × 8.23 m (58 × 27 ft) nave that leads to the approximately 5.79 × 5.33 m (19 × 17.5 ft) chancel. The transepts of the cruciform are formed by two separate areas on either side of the chancel: a sacristy and a choir area (Historic American Buildings Survey 1936). Wooden truss arches support the ceiling and add to the overall vertical appearance of the structure (Figure 2.3). The most significant changes to the interior were the removal of white plaster that originally covered the interior walls and the removal of the gallery once used by the enslaved peoples who attended church services.

FIGURE 2.3. Interior of St. Luke's Episcopal Church. The elevated ceilings and lancet chancel windows highlight the church's vertical space, one of the hallmarks of Gothic Revival architecture. (Photograph by Kimberly Pyszka.)

As with other forms of material culture that people produce and archaeologists study, the architecture, design, and furnishings of St. Luke's Episcopal Church provide us with information about the designers' beliefs and goals. In the following sections I explore the architectural and landscape decisions made by St. Luke's designers and how they expressed the prevailing ideologies within the Episcopal Church, the Diocese of Alabama, the designers' own identities and goals, and those of the broader white Cahaba community.

GOTHIC REVIVAL ARCHITECTURE AND THE PROTESTANT EPISCOPAL CHURCH

In the years immediately following the Revolutionary War, Anglicans in the United States separated from the Church of England and formed the Protestant Episcopal Church. Although they became two distinct organizations, their religious beliefs and ideologies remained very similar, as did the material ways they expressed them. Therefore, ideological changes and subsequent modifications to the material culture that occurred within one organization were often reflected in the other. In the early 1800s, the roots for significant ideological changes within the Church of England emerged that eventually led to a revival of many pre-Reformation beliefs and rituals. Materially, this return to more High Church ideology is reflected through elaborate interior furnishings and decorations, a return to the altar as the main focal point, and a revival of the ornate and extravagant nature of Gothic architecture, especially its emphasis on elevated ceilings and overall structure height.

At that time, two closely related movements began within the Church of England. Both called for a return to the more Catholic-leaning High Church ideology over the Low Church thinking of the eighteenth-century Church we have noted at St. Paul's Parish Church and in early colonial South Carolina more generally. These movements grew out of three primary concerns: that the Church of England had become too secular, an aversion to Classical architecture for being too secular and pagan in nature, and a wish to return to a more formal liturgy and grand visual appearance (Stanton 1997:xviii–xix).

Leaders of the Oxford Movement, many of whom were associated with Oxford University, thought that the Church of England had leaned too Protestant, or Low Church, during the eighteenth century. While they did not desire a full return to the Roman Catholic Church, followers of this movement argued that the Church of England should return to more of a High Church philosophy, especially in regard to its greater emphasis on the ritual and ceremonial aspects of the mass. In particular, the Oxford Movement sought "the greater frequency of the celebration of the Holy Communion, liturgical experiment, more ornate ceremonial, the practice of 'sacramental' confession, the foundation of the theological colleges, . . . the renewal of the monastic life" (Neill 1958:259). As a result, the Church of England, as well as the Episcopal Church, moved in the direction of a stronger connection to the Roman Catholic Church, one that continues to this day.

Similarly, the ecclesiologist movement argued for a return of High Church elements to the Church of England. Followers of this movement, which originated with the Cambridge Camden Society (later called the Ecclesiological Society) at Cambridge University, focused on church architecture and the overall visual appearance of churches rather than on rituals. In particular, they sought a return to the altar, rather than the pulpit, as the focal point of the interior space. This movement grew out of the belief that Gothic architecture had "true Christian roots," unlike the Georgian architecture commonly used in Low churches, which had its origins in the paganism of ancient Greece (Lane 2012:252).

Supporters of both the Oxford and ecclesiologist movements looked toward England's pre-Reformation Gothic churches for inspiration. As a result, Gothic Revival architecture with its more ornate features became the standard within the Church of England and, consequently, the Episcopal Church in the former colonies (Gundersen 1987:260; Perrin 1961:40; Smith 1995; Stanton 1997). The emphasis on height and elevation is particularly symbolic as religious structures around the world, both today and in the past, are often some of the tallest buildings or monuments in their vicinity. From an ideological point of view, such elevation symbolizes, among other things, the proximity of the believers to the heavens and the supernatural. Specific to the Gothic Revival, Augustus Pugin, an English architect and one of the movement's leaders, considered height to be "an expression of the Resurrection" (Stanton 1997:21). More practically, the height of religious structures and/or their location on elevated areas also allows them to be easily seen on the landscape by both followers and nonfollowers alike.

The Cambridge Camden Society had missionary aspirations and was largely responsible for bringing the ecclesiological movement to the United States. Gothic characteristics first appeared on American churches after 1800; however, they still retained several characteristics of Georgian and Classical architecture, particularly their symmetry. By the mid-nineteenth century, newly constructed churches were more accurate examples of Gothic. The symmetry that defined the Georgian and Classical styles was gone, and where available, stone replaced bricks as the primary construction material (Stanton 1997:3). In the United States, Gothic Revival architecture peaked in popularity between 1830 and 1860 (Perrin 1961:40). While best known for its churches, Gothic Revival was also found in residences and other structures. It even influenced other forms of material culture, such as ceramics and other household furnishings (Fitts 1999:47). One of the earliest and finest examples of a "true" Gothic Revival church is Trinity Church in New York City, constructed between 1839 and 1846 and designed by architecture Richard Upjohn (Gundersen 1987:260).

A vast majority of nineteenth-century Gothic Revival churches in the United States belonged to the Episcopal Church, largely due to it pairing well with Episcopalian liturgy and return to High Church ideology. Unlike eighteenth-century Protestant organizations, including the Anglican Church at the time, which stressed the auditory aspects of services and the spoken word of the religious leader, the nineteenth-century Episcopal Church focused on the visual. For Episcopalians, the building itself was a part of the experience of the worship service. Church architecture provided the necessary backdrop to highlight the liturgy, which allowed for architecture and the liturgy to complement and reinforce each other (McNair 2015:74). The building, its furnishings, and its architectural features were meant to awaken all the senses, but especially the visual. Dark interiors contrasted with and highlighted stained-glass windows, high ceilings drew the eyes upward toward Heaven, and colorful exterior fabrics and furnishings and ornate elaborate architectural features on both the exterior and interior were all meant to "arouse the senses, lift the worshipper from ordinary experiences of life and prepare the congregation for the mysteries of Christian rituals" (Lane 2012:258). Additionally, the ornate and elaborate furnishings symbolized offerings and financial sacrifice to God (Smith 1995:74).

Gothic Revival architecture was first found mainly in urban areas, but by the mid-nineteenth century it had begun to spread into rural, frontier areas (Smith 1995:71). By the early 1850s, Gothic Revival churches appeared in Alabama, first in the larger cities of Montgomery, Huntsville, and Mobile, then later in more rural areas, such as Cahaba (McNair 2015:14). The popularity of Gothic Revival architecture and its spread into less urban areas are largely credited to architect Richard Upjohn (Lane 2012:254). A native of England, Upjohn moved to the United States in 1829 and became well known for his Gothic Revival churches, in particular New York City's Trinity Church. Upjohn's preference for Gothic Revival architecture is largely due to identifying himself as a High Church Episcopalian. He designed most of his churches to reflect the ideologies of the Oxford Movement and the Cambridge Camden Society (Gundersen 1987:260–261; Smith 1995). In 1852 Upjohn published his "Wooden Church" plans in *Upjohn's Rural Architecture: Designs, Working Drawings and Specifications for a Wooden Church, and Other Rural Structures*

(1975 [c1852]). His plan is considered the prototype of the Carpenter Gothic architectural style, especially for churches. The publication of *Rural Architecture* allowed architects, church leaders, and carpenters to easily access his designs to use and modify as they saw fit.

Originating with the Gothic Revival designs from northeastern church architects, especially those in New York and in New England, Carpenter Gothic ultimately spread to other areas of the United States. It was especially prevalent in frontier and rural areas of the Midwest and parts of the South, including several in Alabama (Gundersen 1987:259; Lane 2012:249). The style was particularly well-suited to the context of the developing areas of the expanding United States. Stone and brick, the typical construction materials of Gothic and Gothic Revival structures, were often limited in newly acquired lands. Timber, however, was readily available. Consequently, wood became the primary construction material of the Carpenter Gothic, used for both framing and exterior siding. Upjohn also recognized that in rural areas the skill levels of local carpenters and craftsmen varied greatly. Therefore, he supported modifications to his published plans in *Rural Architecture* and encouraged rural churches to design their churches with their own distinct and unique features (Lane 2012:254; Smith 1995). For local church leaders, this flexibility allowed them to express their own ideologies and goals, as well as address issues of the larger community or even region. For example, many of Minnesota's Episcopal churches lacked some of the more ornamental features of the Gothic Revival, such as false buttresses, reflecting the more moderate High church thinking of their congregations (Gundersen 1987:263).

ST. LUKE'S ARCHITECTURE AND THE MATERIALIZATION OF IDEOLOGIES

For the reasons stated, at the time when many local communities began construction on their individual churches Gothic Revival was the primary architectural style of choice for mid-nineteenth-century churches within the Episcopal Diocese of Alabama. Despite the relatively frontier conditions throughout most of the state, Alabama's Episcopal churches reflected the High Church style and furnishings ordinarily found in urban areas (McNair 2015:13). Carpenter Gothic churches were widespread across the state, including the Episcopal churches of St. Andrew's (Prairieville), St. Paul's (Magnolia Springs), Grace Episcopal (Mt. Meigs), St. Paul's (Lowndesboro), Grace Episcopal (Clayton), St. Luke's (Jacksonville), St. Paul's (Mobile) St. John's (Forkland), and St. Luke's (Cahaba). At the same time, while these churches reflected the larger Episcopalian beliefs current at the time, they also mirrored more localized social ideologies. For example, at St. Luke's, building committee members Perine, Mitchell, and Hunter along with Cumming, the contractor they hired, drew largely from Upjohn's plans. However, they did not follow his plans exactly, and by analyzing the differences between their plan and Upjohn's models, it is possible to explore the local ideology they wished to express to their parishioners, other area residents, both free and enslaved, and Cahaba visitors.

Spatially, St. Luke's overall dimensions and its use of vertical space were larger than Upjohn's rural wooden church. At just under 23.77 m (78 ft) in length, St. Luke's was approximately 1.83 m (6 ft) longer. To account for the additional length, the overall width of St. Luke's was also increased by 1.83 m (6 ft). This increased space was added to the floor plan, with both the nave and chancel being larger than indicated in Upjohn's plans. Other modifications to Upjohn's designs led to a greater vertical appearance, starting with the structure's 1.52 m (5 ft) aboveground brick foundations. With the added height of the foundation, 5.18 m (17 ft) high interior walls, a ceiling peak that reached to 11.58 m (38 ft), and its bell tower with spire, St. Luke's extended 27.43 m (90 ft) into the air, a full 3.66 m (12 ft) above Upjohn's plans (Historic American Buildings Survey 1936).

Besides its size and vertical emphasis, St. Luke's varied in other ways from Upjohn's "Wooden Church." One of the more obvious external differences was the addition of exterior buttresses along the nave walls. Although buttresses were common features in Gothic Revival churches, they were not as common within the Carpenter Gothic style; nor were they a part of Upjohn's design. These buttresses provided additional support to the structure while also giving a more ornate feel to the church's exterior. Cumming also added double windows to the nave's exterior walls rather than the single ones Upjohn called for. Another exterior difference concerned the steeple that rose from their respective bell towers. Although today's St. Luke's is missing its steeple, consulting the 1872 drawing of the church by A. M. Vasser reveals that St. Luke's steeple did not have the clean lines that Upjohn envisioned (see Figure 2.2). Instead, Vasser depicted a spire that resembled a "magnified candle snuffer" (Upjohn 1939:120).

Variations can also be seen in St. Luke's interior. Unlike Upjohn's plans, St. Luke's at one point had a second-floor gallery that worshippers accessed through a staircase located in the bell tower. It also has an additional chancel extension, which housed a choir transept opposite the vestry (or sacristy). Although dark stained wooden interiors were common with Carpenter Gothic churches, at St. Luke's the interior walls were once covered in white plaster (Dallas Gazette March 31, 1854). Along with the added natural light from the nave's extra windows, the white walls would have made for a very bright interior, unlike the dark interiors typically found in Gothic Revival and Carpenter Gothic churches. The design choices made by Cumming and the building committee members altered Upjohn's "Wooden Church" into *their* wooden church. In addition to expressing the High Church ideas of the Episcopal Church and that of the Diocese of Alabama, St. Luke's also reflected local conditions and influences, both environmental and social.

Environmental conditions likely factored into one of more obvious differences seen at St. Luke's when compared with Upjohn's plans—its 1.52 m aboveground foundation. Flood waters from the Alabama and Cahaba Rivers often impacted the town (and continue to affect the park today). Officials considered their past experiences with rising flood waters as they planned St. Luke's. At its original location on Vine Street, the church stood approximately 100 m west of the Alabama River, a spot with little elevation rise between the river and structure. Additionally, a ravine along the north side of the church allowed floodwaters to potentially encroach within feet of the building. From floods in the past, Cahaba residents knew the lot on which St. Luke's would stand would be prone to occasional flooding. Therefore, unlike Upjohn's design with only minimal aboveground foundations, St. Luke's foundations stood approximately 1.5 m above the ground surface. Although the main purpose of these tall foundations was to raise the church enough off the ground to protect it from flooding, the additional height also had the added benefit of increasing the structure's verticality, making St. Luke's one of the most visible features on the cultural landscape.

Other design decisions are attributable to the area's natural resources. In urban areas, Gothic Revival churches were often constructed of stone or brick. However, as seen in other nonurban churches, Cumming and local carpenters took advantage of the abundance of timber in the Cahaba area and used wood as the primary construction material throughout the church. One of the most distinctive features of Carpenter Gothic churches is the board-and-batten siding that covers exterior walls, and St. Luke's follows that model. Although today a metal roof protects the church, originally wooden shingles did. Inside the church, wood was used for everything from the floor to the peak of the 11.58 m (38 ft) ceiling.

St. Luke's designers took into consideration the various environmental conditions and availability of local resources as they planned their church, but cultural and social factors also played a large role in their decision-making. In the early 1850s, no single social issue in the United States was as contentious as whether or not any individual had the right to own another individual. Slavery had already been outlawed in many states by this time, but it continued to thrive in the South. Despite many of Cahaba's wealthiest and most influential citizens being from the Northeast, locally slavery remained an important component of their individual prosperity, as well as that of Cahaba, Dallas County, Alabama, and the entire South.

The social beliefs of St. Luke's building committee members, the congregation, and the Cahaba community regarding racial identity, slavery, and segregation were all materially expressed through the addition of a gallery (removed in 1878). Galleries were not common features of Episcopal churches: ecclesiologists tried to avoid them as they created an architectural divide within the church's interior that also physically separated congregation members (McNair 2017:115). Upjohn did not call for them in his plans, either. However, galleries featured commonly among Alabama's Episcopal churches and many other churches throughout the South. One of the main reasons for the addition of galleries in the South is that they provided a separate space for enslaved worshippers during church services. Although church leaders, white enslavers, and society in general sought for the conversion of enslaved Africans and their descendants to Christianity, they still desired to maintain a socially approved distance from them.

In another deviation from Upjohn's plan, St. Luke's had two separate entrances—one for white parishioners and the other for Black parishioners—that created an additional architectural barrier between its Black and white parishioners. To accommodate the local desire for separate spaces, Cumming moved the church's primary entrance to the structure's western gabled end and placed the steeple tower to its left (McNair 2017:115–116). The main entrance led directly into the nave, where only white parishioners were allowed. Black parishioners entered the church through a second entrance located at the base of the steeple tower. Once inside, a staircase guided them to their designated space in the gallery and did not allow them access to the nave or other parts of the edifice. The separate entrance eliminated or greatly reduced any contact between Black and white parishioners.

The addition of a second entrance and gallery at St. Luke's was a local adaptation to Upjohn's design. By creating distinct spaces within the church, building committee members materially expressed the dominant white social ideology of the time and region related to slavery and the separation of people of different racial backgrounds. For St. Luke's white parishioners, the segregation of Black parishioners reinforced their own dominance and authority, both within the church walls themselves and the larger society. They likely wanted to remind Black parishioners that they were distinct, not considered to truly be a part of the congregation, and that they were not to associate with white parishioners. As white people were a minority of the Cahaba community's population, they likely felt the need to express their power and authority over the Black majority. Of course, just because that is what they desired to express does not mean that the Black community accepted the intended messages or responded in the ways expected. I revisit this idea in chapter 4.

Another consideration of the material expressions of St. Luke's relates to the Reverend Cushman's 1854 description of the newly consecrated church as "an edifice which is an ornament to the diocese as well as to the Parish" (Protestant Episcopal Church, Diocese of Alabama 1854:12). His description of St. Luke's as an "ornament" tells us that to Cushman and parishioners, the church was much more than simply a structure to hold worship services and practice their religious beliefs in—St. Luke's was meant to be a showcase. It was intended to convey meaning. But what were the intended messages?

For Episcopalians in general, church design reflected the sacrifices, including financial, of parishioners (Smith 1995:74). For those members of Cahaba's wealthiest families belonging to the Episcopal Church, St. Luke's was an expression of not only their sacrifices to God but also of their wealth and social standing in Cahaba and the surrounding area. Especially in nonurban areas, the Gothic elements of Alabama's Gothic Revival churches, so unlike any other structure in the community, made them "a symbol of refinement and wealth" (McNair 2015:14). As described, St. Luke's was purposely built to be larger than Upjohn's "Wooden Church." The overall scale was one way for its designers and parishioners to express their social status as it showed that they had the necessary funds and other resources to construct such a large building. The church's size also represented their belief that St. Luke's congregation, as well as Cahaba's population, would continue to grow.

In addition to its grand scale, St. Luke's stained-glass windows also represented the social status and wealth of its parishioners. On its own, the presence of stained-glass windows was not unusual for a mid-nineteenth-century Episcopalian church. Such windows added to the beauty and visual appearance of the church and reflected its High Church ideology. At the same time, stained-glass windows were more expensive than clear windows and, therefore, can be understood as a way for the local congregation to visually communicate their social wealth (Smith 1995:85).

When comparing the number of stained-glass windows at St. Luke's to Upjohn's specifications, St. Luke's had twenty windows compared to Upjohn's twelve, not including the triple chancel windows. Most of the difference was due to the double windows that lined either side of the nave at St. Luke's (Upjohn's design depicted single windows). Furthermore, while today St. Luke's three chancel windows are colorless glass, the original ones were stained glass and can be found at St. Andrew's Episcopal Church in Prairieville. A comparison of Upjohn's plans to the HABS drawings of St. Luke's and St. Andrew's shows that the chancel windows were larger than Upjohn envisioned. St. Luke's center window was slightly wider, measuring 0.91 × 3.76 m (3 ft × 12 ft 4 in) compared to Upjohn's 0.91 × 2.9 m (3 ft × 9 ft 6 in). However, the triplet's two side windows were notably larger both in width and length—0.61 × 2.64 m (2 ft × 8 ft 8 in) compared to Upjohn's 0.41 × 1.52 m (1 ft 4 in × 5 ft). By using more windows than Upjohn called for and larger ones in the chancel, St. Luke's designers may have intentionally used the more expensive stained-glass windows as a means to materially express their wealth and social status.

In addition to reflecting wealth and status, St. Luke's relatively grand design had some architectural features that were more reminiscent of urban churches, which consciously or not reflected the northeastern roots of many of its parishioners. In 1995 Smith studied the dozen or so Episcopal churches along the St. John's River on Florida's eastern coast. In describing the churches, Smith notes that "they enunciate an important historical relationship with northeastern peoples and ideas. They were built on the river's banks, blending local materials and demands with nationally known Gothic Revival architecture. Specifically, they represent the wooden adaptation of Gothic known as Carpenter Gothic, expressed in their vertical lines, board-and-batten siding, and stained glass" (Smith 1995:67–68). Smith could have just as easily been describing St. Luke's Episcopal Church. Another parallel to St. Luke's is that the St. John's River Episcopal churches followed Upjohn's "Wooden Church" design, but with local alterations to reflect the natural resources of Florida as well as the preferences of local congregations (Smith 1995:86). The parallels between Cahaba's St. Luke's and the Florida churches are further strengthened due to similarities in the makeup of parishioners and other local residents. Both in Cahaba and the river communities along the St. John's River, local Episcopalians used church architecture to reflect their northeastern roots as well as their wealth.

Specifically, using two of the St. John's River area churches as primary case studies—St. Mary's in Green Cove Springs (1879) and St. George's of Fort George Island (1883)—Smith wrote that the churches reflected the northern culture that was (and in many ways still is) a part of Florida's society and culture (1995:68). They achieved this by following architectural trends popular in the Northeast, in particular Gothic Revival architecture that made its first appearance in the United States in that region (Smith 1995:74). Unlike Cahaba's residents, many parishioners along the St. John's River were "snowbirds," who spent their winters in Florida and the remainder of the year back home (Lane 2012:250; Smith 1995). In their case, having churches that were "recognizable products of northern design and ideology" helped them to feel more at home while they wintered in Florida (Smith 1995:88).

Although Carpenter Gothic churches were found elsewhere in Alabama, St. Luke's stands out due to its overall size, the exterior buttresses, elaborate stained-glass windows, and exaggerated verticality. These architectural and design elements led it to being more reminiscent of northeastern urban Gothic Revival churches and less like the other churches of mid-nineteenth-century Central Alabama or other more rural or frontier areas. St. Luke's expressed the social status and wealth of its white parishioners, local beliefs regarding slavery, the social hierarchy between white and Black residents, and the northeastern backgrounds of many of its parishioners. For the larger geographic community, St. Luke's visual appearance provided Cahaba with a more cosmopolitan and urban feel. It was a material expression of the community's belief and confidence that their town would continue to flourish and remain an important part of Dallas County, Central Alabama, and the South—economically, politically, and socially.

ST. LUKE'S LANDSCAPE AND THE MATERIALIZATION OF IDEOLOGIES

In addition to making architectural decisions at St. Luke's that materially expressed their religious and social ideology and their goals for both their church and the Cahaba community, St. Luke's leaders also made decisions about how best to utilize the landscape to express those same beliefs. Despite 150 years and nearly 500 miles separating the two churches, many parallels can be made between St. Luke's and St. Paul's Parish Church discussed in the previous chapter. With both churches, designers took advantage of natural and cultural landscape features to showcase their respective churches. Additionally, strategic placement on the landscape magnified some of their architectural features. In the case of St. Luke's, this combination of architectural and landscape choices led to the church being a visual focal point on the landscape to those traveling along or approaching Cahaba from the Alabama River, as well as to people in the town itself.

Today St. Luke's sits across the road from the park's Visitor's Center, nearly 1,000 m from the banks of the Alabama River. However, when first constructed it sat a mere 100 m from the water. Maps, memoirs, and other historical documents indicate St. Luke's was originally constructed on a lot at the intersection of Vine and First South Streets. Through archaeological excavations, Cahaba's park manager and archaeologist Linda Derry identified the exact location and positioning of the church on that lot. These excavations took place in 1986 as part of an archaeological survey of the then 24-acre park, focusing on the area of Cahaba's original town center. The primary goal of the survey was to identify any archaeologically significant areas in order to avoid them in the planning and construction of park facilities. This systematic survey, which included 0.76 m² (2.5 ft²) test units placed every 12.19 m (40 ft), identified several areas that warranted further archaeological testing. Later that year, the Alabama State Museum of Natural History's Expedition program joined Derry and her crew to further investigate these areas. They identified several prehistoric features, the location of Castle Morgan (a Civil War Confederate prison), and the original location of St. Luke's Episcopal Church (Derry 2000:19). Derry's excavations uncovered linear changes in soil color, marking the location of brick foundation trenches (Figure 2.4). The dimensions of these trenches matched those of the extant church, which at the time still stood in Martin's Station, verifying that this site was indeed the original location of St. Luke's Episcopal Church. Derry's excavations also provided visual evidence of the church's exact positioning on the landscape. Like the entire town grid itself, St. Luke's orientation was shifted approximately twenty-five degrees south of true east. Due to this shift, the church's main entrance, the west gable end, directly faced Vine Street, while its east gable end overlooked the Alabama River. With its location and positioning,

FIGURE 2.4. Archaeological excavations at the original site of St. Luke's Episcopal Church, 1986. The original foundation trench is seen along the right side of excavation block. (Photograph courtesy of Linda Derry, Old Cahawba Archaeological Park.)

St. Luke's was a prominent fixture of Cahaba's cultural landscape, both to those who saw it from the land and to those who noticed it from the river.

Although St. Luke's was constructed over thirty years later, an analysis of its placement within the cultural landscape of 1850s Cahaba begins with the town's 1818 founding. After Governor Bibb's successful attempt to have Cahawba declared the state capital, the entire town needed to be carved from the Alabama wilderness. But first, Bibb needed to sell town lots. To that end, Bibb developed Cahawba—on paper. In the style of many other southern frontier communities, Cahawba was very much a planned town from its start (Derry 2000:16–17). Specifically, Bibb commissioned a map of Cahawba to be drawn to show perspective buyers a developed town (Figure 2.5). The envisioned town was situated on 1,620 acres between the Alabama and Cahaba Rivers and was divided into several blocks with named streets running between them. Each of the blocks contained four and a half acre lots, with fourteen blocks running one direction and six blocks the other (Scott 2011:15). While it was common to have town grids laid out in the cardinal directions, Cahawba's street grid was not on true north-south and east-west axes. Instead, Bibb shifted it approximately 25 degrees. This alteration meant Vine Street, the primary north-south road, would run parallel to the Alabama River, while the west-east Capital Street sat perpendicular to the waterway. Such an orientation would make the town more visible from the Alabama River to passersby.

Bibb also took advantage of the already existing cultural landscape. On the map of his planned town, a semicircular lot along the west bank of the Alabama River stands out among the otherwise perfectly squared off grid of streets and town blocks, surrounded by the appropriately named Arch Street. A large building is seen in the center of the lot, presumably Bibb's planned statehouse. What neither Bibb's planned town map nor today's landscape tells us is that the unique semicircle lot was already a part of the cultural landscape. Through archaeological excavations, we now know that a late prehistoric Native American burial mound with a surrounding moat and palisade once stood in this very spot (Knight 1987). Based on Bibb's map, the moat would have aligned with Arch Street, which explains the unusual semicircular feature in comparison to the rest of the town grid. Archaeological evidence indicates the moat was visible on the Cahawba landscape until the late 1850s, when it was filled (Derry 2000:24). Apparently, Bibb planned to take advantage of the existing mound and moat to highlight his proposed statehouse. Placed on the mound, it would have sat at a higher elevation than the surrounding buildings and easily would have been the most prominent building seen by people traveling the Alabama River. This location would

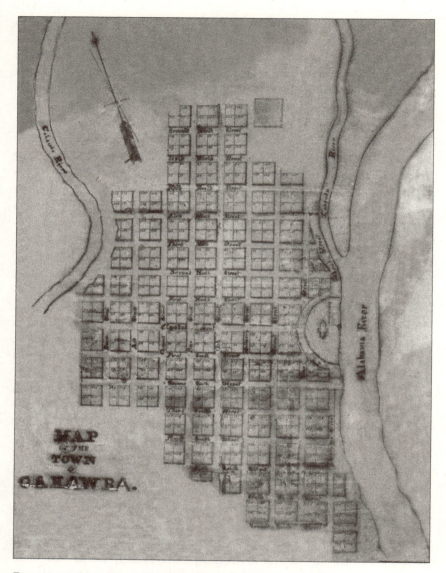

FIGURE 2.5. Original map of the town of Cahawba. Governor Bibb commissioned an unknown artist to create this map of the envisioned capital town. Bibb's planned statehouse is visible within the semicircle lot along the banks of the Alabama River. (Map adapted by Linda Derry, Old Cahawba Archaeological Park, from "Map of the Town of Cahawba" on file with the Alabama Department of Archives and History. Courtesy of Linda Derry, Old Cahawba Archaeological Park, and Alabama Department of Archives and History.)

have also made it the most noticeable structure for people living, working, and visiting the town. Situated on the elevated lot at the terminus of Capital Street, one of the town's main streets, the statehouse would have certainly drawn the eye of all.

Besides making the statehouse the highlight of the cultural landscape the intent to build the new Alabama statehouse atop a Native American mound was also a way to materially express European American power and control over the land. This physical representation would have been especially important in those initial years following the Creek War of 1813–1814, which resulted in the ceding of Creek lands that included much of Central Alabama, including Cahawba. Had it been built, Bibb's statehouse would have served as a materialization of the ideology of the dominant group—the white settlers who now had control over former Creek lands—and the power of the newly formed state to back up that control. Still, Bibb's vision never came to fruition. The state legislature did not approve the funds necessary for his grand statehouse. Instead, a temporary statehouse was constructed on a lot that sat across Arch Street from Bibb's proposed location (Roark 1985; Scott 2011:16). In preparation for Alabama's bicentennial in December 2019, the AHC conducted archaeological excavations at the temporary statehouse location. While these excavations do not directly relate to St. Luke's Episcopal Church, their results show the extent Cahawba officials went to design their developing town around the cultural landscape—in this case, the late prehistoric moat.

During these excavations, AHC archaeologists uncovered the builders' trench and in situ portions of the statehouse's brick walls, which provided an outline of the former statehouse and later Dallas County courthouse. Surprisingly, the building was not rectangular or even square-shaped. Instead, it was trapezoidal-shaped, with its south wall extending farther to the east than the north wall, resulting in the east wall being at a different angle from the rest of the structure. A trapezoid-shaped building is unusual even today but would have been especially so during the early nineteenth century, at a time when Federal architecture with its strict symmetry was the standard. However, this unconventional shape made it possible for the entire front façade of the statehouse to face Arch Street directly. By taking advantage of the existing Native American cultural landscape that surrounded the late prehistoric moat and mound, those involved in the design and construction of the statehouse intentionally constructed their structure to align with the existing cultural landscape to ensure that it was a prominent part of Cahawba's landscape, especially for those who traveled along Arch or Capitol Streets (Sipes and Derry 2019).

While the Cahaba River was a factor in Cahawba's initial settlement and its later growth and prosperity, the Alabama River played a more vital role. Proximity to the Alabama was one of the reasons Governor Bibb lobbied for this particular location to serve as the state capital. In the early days of the settlement, it provided ease of travel for potential residents, visitors, and state politicians, especially at a time when roads were still few and few between. It also allowed for the delivery of necessary supplies as the town was being built out of the wilderness. Later, as cotton production began to boom in the region, the river provided planters an easy way to ship their product to Selma, Montgomery, and most importantly, to Mobile's ports where Dallas County cotton could be shipped throughout the world. At the height of Cahaba's prosperity, the Alabama River also brought goods for local merchants to sell in their stores and visitors to occupy local hotels. Every day, people arrived to or traveled by Cahaba via the Alabama. While Governor Bibb envisioned the statehouse as the most prominent building they saw from the river, for St. Luke's leaders and parishioners, it was their church that should be the most visible.

In the quotation that opens this chapter, St. Luke's Reverend Cushman noted that St. Luke's "architectural beauty" drew attention. In the same text, he remarked that its position along the Alabama River placed it "in sight of all the travel upon that thoroughfare" (Cushman 1854:252). Similar to St. Paul's Parish Church, St. Luke's was oriented so that parishioners faced more east to east-southeast than the traditional "true" east. Both churches would have been easily visible from their respective nearby waterways, if in somewhat different ways. At St. Paul's, leaders made the decision to situate their church on the landscape so that its long axis faced the Stono River, making it as visible as possible from the water. At St. Luke's, its more narrow, gabled end faced the Alabama River. With this placement on the landscape, its front façade overlooked Vine Street, a major thoroughfare, while parishioners still sat facing in an easterly direction. At the same time, St. Luke's had two distinguishing features that helped it to otherwise visually stand out that St. Paul's did not: a bell tower and the triplet of stained-glass windows along its eastern wall.

St. Luke's 27.43 m (90 ft) tall bell tower and spire truly made the church a focal point of Cahaba's landscape. As the town's tallest structure, it would have been one of the first, if not the first, visible features of the town. It also likely served as a landmark to river travelers to let them know they were nearing Cahaba. Whether they docked in town or continued their journey up the Alabama River, St. Luke's large, triple stained-glass windows also probably caught travelers' eyes, drawing attention to the church and, thus, the town.

From the land vantage point, St. Luke's was also a focal point for residents and visitors alike. Located immediately across Vine Street from the Dallas County courthouse (the former location of the statehouse), St. Luke's occupied a portion of the town's main square. Although there were other churches present in Cahaba, only St. Luke's stood in the town's center. Its prime location expressed the importance of the Episcopal Church, its leaders, and its congregation to the entire community. Whether from land or water, St. Luke's Episcopal Church was a conspicuous, prominent feature of the cultural landscape and expressed the prominent role of the Episcopal Church in the town and the wealth and importance of its leaders and parishioners, many of whom were prosperous planters, merchants, and businessmen.

In a number of ways, St. Luke's Episcopal Church's architecture expressed the religious, social, and cultural ideologies of the Protestant Episcopal Church, St. Luke's white parishioners, and of Cahaba itself. Its Gothic Revival architecture and relatively ornate design features—namely its emphasis on vertical lines of site, buttresses, numerous stained-glass windows, and its overall dimensions—materially expressed the beliefs and goals of all three, while its strategic placement on the landscape magnified its visual appearance from both land and water.

As a consequence, the decisions made by St. Luke's leaders aided in unifying white church members behind their common identities, namely as wealthy, white, Episcopalians, many with northeastern roots. Their decisions also united townspeople, even those who were not Episcopalian, around their goals of presenting Cahaba as a modern, cosmopolitan town, despite its relatively remote location. In chapter 4, I explore these ideas regarding the formation and strengthening of community identity in more detail; for now, I shift focus to a different type of religious structure—Cane Hill College in northwestern Arkansas.

CHAPTER THREE

Cane Hill College, Cane Hill, Arkansas

> We owe it to ourselves and to God to kindle a light on this hilltop which will over-top all surrounding hills and mountains, and bear intelligence and lights and gladness on the wings of its beams far off to distant regions.
>
> —Professor Samuel Doak Lowry, Cane Hill, Arkansas, June 23, 1835

In May 2017 the community of Cane Hill hosted a celebration of its 1886 Cane Hill College building. This event followed the completion of a $1.4 million preservation project funded by Historic Cane Hill Inc., the nonprofit that manages the historic community (Figure 3.1). Over a thousand people attended the ribbon-cutting ceremony and toured the restored structure. Many of the people in attendance were there to reminisce about their childhood years spent at Cane Hill School and to share those memories with younger family members. Some individuals attended due to the opportunity to tour the impressive building that is unique to the rural landscape of Washington County. Others joined in the festivities to remember a large part of the community's past—one centered on the Cumberland Presbyterians who founded the town and Cane Hill College. No matter their reason for attending, everyone was there to celebrate the building, remember its past, and imagine the possibilities the future holds for it.

FIGURE 3.1. Cane Hill College 1886 building, in 2017, shortly after completion of renovation project. (Photograph by Kimberly Pyszka.)

The Cumberland Presbyterians who established Cane Hill in 1827 held education to be a vital part of their religious beliefs and teachings.[1] It is unsurprising, therefore, that education stood at the center of their plans for the community from its inception with the establishment of a school circa 1834, followed by the founding of Cane Hill College in 1852. In large part due to the college, Cane Hill prospered throughout the nineteenth century and was home to multiple general stores, a bank, a hotel, a Methodist church, and three separate Cumberland Presbyterian congregations. However, by the late 1800s Cane Hill began a steady decline, largely as a result of the refusal of town leaders and residents to allow the railroad to pass through their community. That decline continued throughout the twentieth century (Braly 2019). Cane Hill College, which closed its doors in 1891, witnessed this evolution from its hillside location on the town's western edge.

Although it has been several decades since students last sat in its classrooms, the former college building remains the visual and social center of Cane Hill and a source of pride for area residents. It is also a material reminder of the town's founding Cumberland Presbyterians and their emphasis on education. Still, the current building was not constructed until 1886, over fifty years after the Cumberland Presbyterians founded their first school. At least three previous structures, in two separate locations, are known through documentary and now archaeological evidence.

While not a church or specifically a place of worship, Cane Hill College is still a building that holds religious significance and meaning. Cumberland Presbyterians founded and oversaw all aspects of the college, and the college's primary goal was to educate and prepare young men for the ministry. Cane Hill College was a place where Cumberland Presbyterian ideology was taught, practiced, and upheld. Additionally, based on historical accounts, the successive college buildings had large rooms that served as chapels, not only for students but for members of the larger community as well. The buildings were designed by the college's board of trustees, all members of the Cumberland Presbyterian Church, and the names of recorded contractors include several church members (Campbell 1985:49). Therefore, it is expected that their religious ideology and goals would be expressed through a variety of decisions they made, including the location and overall visual appearance of the college. In this chapter, I examine the landscape choices the Cumberland Presbyterians made in regard to the location of their buildings, how those decisions materially expressed their emphasis on education, and how the college helped to strengthen Cumberland Presbyterian identity and spread the associated values to residents of the larger geographic community.

CUMBERLAND PRESBYTERIANS IN CANE HILL

To fully comprehend the importance of education, specifically higher education, to Cane Hill's Cumberland Presbyterians, one needs to begin with an understanding of the Cumberland split from the larger Presbyterian Church. There were doctrinal differences, in particular the Cumberlands' rejection of the Presbyterian Church's Calvinist idea of predestination. Instead, Cumberland Presbyterians believed that rather than their salvation being predetermined by God, one's actions throughout their lifetime would be the determinant (Gage 2006:8–9). There were also disagreements regarding education requirements of ministers. As my discussion focuses on Cane Hill College and the importance of education to Cumberland Presbyterians, the following historical overview of the Cumberland Presbyterian Church's beginnings concentrates on these educational requirements.[2]

In the late eighteenth century, a revival movement known as the Second Great Awakening spread westward into the frontier areas of the newly formed and expanding United States. One of the main messages of the Second Great Awakening was that individuals had free will over their actions and therefore, over their own salvation. Especially in frontier areas where religious teaching and practices had waned, white settlers welcomed the revival movement. Among other things, this revival movement resulted in a significant increase in Presbyterian membership and, consequently, a need for additional ministers. However, in frontier areas, finding men to fill this need was difficult (Barrus et al. 1972). In addition to a willingness to serve, the Presbyterian Church required its ministers to have a "classical education," by which it meant that men applying for the ministry should have graduated from a college or university located in Europe or the East Coast. Additionally, the curriculum must have included a variety of math and sciences, logic and philosophy courses, grammar and rhetoric, and readings in Greek and Latin (Barrus et al. 1972:87). Only under extraordinary circumstances would the Presbyterian Church approve one to be a minister without the "proper" education.

By the late 1790s, the revival movement reached Kentucky and Tennessee. The Kentucky Synod, the regional governing body of the Presbyterian Church, had two regional presbyteries—the Transylvania Presbytery and the Cumberland Presbytery, which included southern parts of Kentucky and the Cumberland River Valley area of Tennessee. In the face of the urgent need to provide ministers for their growing membership, in 1803 the Cumberland Presbytery approved a group of men to join the ministry, despite them not having the "classical education" required by the Presbyterian Church. The Cumberland Presbytery argued the immediate need for ministers qualified as an "extraordinary circumstance." Additionally, presbytery leaders contended that these men were indeed educated (if not classically) and were therefore qualified to minister. Disagreements regarding these appointments and the Cumberland Presbytery's rejection of predestination led to several years of dispute between the presbytery and the Kentucky Synod. Unable to reach a mutually acceptable compromise, in October 1813 the Cumberland Presbytery formally split from the Presbyterian Church, founding the Cumberland Synod and becoming formally known as the Cumberland Presbyterian Church (Barrus et al. 1972).

In 1811 members of the Pyeatte and Carnahan families were part of the initial group of Cumberland Presbyterians to settle in Arkansas Territory. Arriving from Kentucky and Tennessee via northern Alabama, they first settled at Arkansas Post, located just west of the Mississippi River, near modern-day Pendleton. These two families would later play a significant part in the establishment and growth of Cane Hill. Among this group was John Carnahan, the patriarch of the Carnahan family and the first Cumberland Presbyterian minister in Arkansas Territory. Carnahan, a circuit rider, preached in the territory as early as 1811 and remained its only ordained Cumberland Presbyterian minister until 1826. A short time later, the Cumberland Presbyterians moved to Crystal Hill, located along the Arkansas River just north of Little Rock. In 1827 several families, including the Pyeattes, Carnahans, and Buchanans, left Crystal Hill for northwestern Arkansas. There they established Cane Hill in Washington County (Campbell 1985:8, 15; Gage 2006:20–24). A year later, they officially organized the Cane Hill Cumberland Presbyterian Church (Campbell 1985:17; Carnahan 1954:8; Ellis 1991).

As part of their commitment to education, within a few years of settling Cane Hill, the Cumberland Presbyterians soon turned their attention to the establishment of a school. No primary sources related to the first school in the community have been identified; however, there are a number of secondary sources that recount its history. While these accounts vary slightly in some details, they agree that by 1834 there was a movement to open a school of higher education to prepare young men for the ministry (Carnahan 1954; Gage 2006:45; Karnes 1985; McCulloch 1989; Richardson 1955). On October 28 of that year, church officials met to establish their school, forming a board of trustees and other officials to oversee it (Campbell 1985:47; Carnahan 1954:9; McCulloch 1989:2). The Reverend Samuel King, one of the founding members of the Cumberland Presbyterian Church, attended this meeting and agreed to serve as its founding chair (Campbell 1985:47). The school opened in early 1835, two years before Arkansas achieved statehood, and it most likely was the first school in the territory. Per these secondary sources, the school building, often referred to as "the old meeting house" in Cumberland Presbyterian records, was a log structure that sat on a hill near the town. These sources also state this hill was the same one where today's Cane Hill Cemetery is located (Carnahan 1954:8; McColloch 1989:1). No aboveground evidence of this building, or any other structure, remains.

In 1844 a second Cumberland Presbyterian congregation, the Salem congregation, formed in the Cane Hill community, with the original congregation now referred to as the Cane Hill congregation. While education was a priority for both congregations, it was the Salem congregation that eventually founded Cane Hill College. The first of two important steps in the growth of the school took place on December 26, 1850. On that date, the Arkansas State Legislature granted the Arkansas and Washington Presbyteries of the Cumberland Presbyterian Church a charter for the school, now called Cane Hill Collegiate Institute (Arkansas State Legislature 1850). That same year, the board of trustees oversaw the erection of a new school building. This building is reported to have been a two-story, two-room brick building, located just west of the community "on top of a limestone-faced hill from which a large spring flowed" (McCulloch 1989:7). Unfortunately, no photographs or other visual evidence of this building survive.

The second important step occurred only two years later, when the state legislature passed another act related to the school. This act approved Cane Hill Collegiate Institute to change its name to Cane Hill College. It also removed the Washington Presbytery from the school, leaving control and management of the school to the Arkansas Synod. Most importantly, the school became the first institution in the state to be authorized to "confer such degrees in arts and sciences upon such other persons, as in their judgment are worth of them, as usually conferred by colleges and universities in the United States" (Arkansas State Legislature 1852a). Although the college only admitted men at the time, just days prior, the legislature passed an act establishing the Cane Hill Female Seminary, also under control of the Arkansas Synod. The Female Seminary was located just south of the men's college, near the present-day community of Clyde (Arkansas State Legislature 1852b).

With official recognition as a college, trustees moved forward with developing the campus around the original 1850 brick structure. In 1854 the college added a second building to its grounds. It reportedly housed an assembly room where church services and other community events were held, a library, a physics laboratory, and classrooms (Basham 1969:141; Campbell 1985:48; Richardson 1955:56). College trustees added yet another building in 1858 at the cost of $6,000. Opening in the fall of 1858, this two-story, 13.1 × 22.86 m (43 × 75 ft) brick building became the main building of the college (Basham 1969:142; Campbell 1985:49). The only known surviving photograph shows little of the structure itself (Figure 3.2). A fourth building served as a dormitory. Although its exact location is unknown, we do know that the dormitory was a two-story, wood-frame I-house, with a two-story front porch. Local lore places it away from the three main campus buildings, but it is unclear as to what the actual distance between them was.

During the late 1850s and early 1860s, enrollment at the college grew. Per the 1858–1859 college catalogue, eighty-eight students attended Cane Hill College during that academic year (Cane Hill College 1859:7). However, just a couple of years later, the outbreak of the Civil War led to the temporary closing of the college, as many of its students and professors, including President Fountain Richard Earle, left to enlist and fight for the Confederacy (Basham 1969:163). Northwest Arkansas saw many Civil War battles and skirmishes as Union troops from Missouri and Confederate troops in Arkansas fought for control of this border region. In November 1862, Union troops from Jennison's brigade, under the command of Brigadier General James Blount, "wantonly destroyed" the college (Committee on War Claims

FIGURE 3.2. Students and professors pose for a photograph in front of the 1858 Cane Hill College building. Date unknown. (Courtesy of Historic Cane Hill Museum.)

1880). Union soldier Robert T. McMahon wrote in his diary that "one [shell] exploded in the room in which was kept Mathematical, Astronomical, Philosophical, Geographic, etc. etc. instruments" (Robert T. McMahon diary, December 7, 1862, University of Missouri-Columbia). The shelling destroyed the three main campus buildings, with only the dormitory left standing.

Using the surviving dormitory for classes, students and professors returned and instruction resumed in 1865. Like many communities throughout the southern states, Cane Hill suffered great losses during the Civil War in the form of lives and property, from which it took several years to recover. Not only were there tremendous expenses involved in terms of recovery and rebuilding but the lack of labor from both war casualties and the loss of enslaved labor also led to delays. The rebuilding of Cane Hill College, therefore, took all of three years, completed in 1868.

The new college building was a two-story, wood-framed structure (Figure 3.3). Records state that it measured 13.1 × 22.85 m (43 × 75 ft) and was constructed over the footprint of the destroyed 1858 main college building. The first floor housed a chapel, while classrooms were located on the second floor (Carnahan 1954:9). Despite their new building, college trustees were unsatisfied as they thought it did not measure up to the standard and quality of the buildings it replaced. In 1880 the Committee on War Claims submitted

FIGURE 3.3. Sketch of the 1868 wood-framed Cane Hill College building. This structure replaced the college buildings destroyed during the Civil War. Date and artist unknown. (Courtesy of Historic Cane Hill Museum.)

a petition on behalf on Cane Hill College for restitution of property lost during the Civil War. In this report, the committee requested $15,000 to assist Cane Hill College in its efforts to recover from losses suffered at the hands of Union troops. The request specifically stated that although a new "cheap building" had been constructed and that over one hundred students now attended the college, "the school is being carried on under great disadvantages by reason of insufficient buildings and the want of a library and apparatus for the use of the pupils" (Committee on War Claims 1880).

Despite the lack of space and resources, Cane Hill College flourished for a few years. During the 1876–1877 academic year, five instructors taught courses to 113 students (Cane Hill College 1877:3–7). Among these students were some of the first women to graduate from any four-year-degree granting institution in Arkansas, after Cane Hill College and the Cane Hill Female Seminary merged in 1875. The college's curriculum was quite rigorous, requiring students to enroll in a variety of math and science courses, including algebra, trigonometry, calculus, chemistry, astronomy, geology, zoology, geography, and physiology. Students were also exposed to a wide range of liberal arts courses such as philosophy, Latin, Greek, history, music, painting, composition, and rhetoric. Special English courses on Virgil, Cicero, Herodotus, Homer, Horace, and Tacitus and a multitude of other courses were offered (Cane Hill College 1877:9–10).

Cane Hill College operated in this building until 1885, when a fire attributed to arson destroyed it. Despite the loss of the building, classes continued as the local Methodist Episcopal Church opened its doors and allowed their church to be used for classrooms (Basham 1969:152; Campbell 1985:49). Just over a year later, a new large, brick Italianate-style college building was inaugurated; it survives to this day (Figure 3.4), situated halfway up a hill on the western edge of the community. As it did in the late nineteenth century, Cane Hill College remains a prominent feature on the landscape (Figure 3.5).

In 1891, only five years after opening this new building, Cane Hill College closed its doors for good; the reasons for this closing are unknown, as no documentation has been found that specifically discusses or announces it (Basham 1969:250–251). That same year, Arkansas Cumberland College opened in Clarksville, with Earle serving as its president. Later renamed the University of the Ozarks, the college remains in operation today. The former Cane Hill College building remained a place for education, as it converted to a public elementary and high school. For several decades, Cane

FIGURE 3.4. Circa 1900 photograph of the 1886 Cane Hill College building. This photograph helped guide renovations in 2016–2017. (Courtesy of Historic Cane Hill Museum.)

FIGURE 3.5. Early twentieth-century view of Cane Hill, facing northwest. The 1886 Cane Hill College building (arrow) sits in its current location, approximately halfway up the hill on the town's western edge. (Courtesy of Historic Cane Hill Museum.)

Hill's children attended school, played sports, were involved in student organizations, and participated in a variety of school functions in the former college building. In the 1940s students in grades 7–12 began to attend the nearby Lincoln School District. In 1956 the last classes were held at the former Cane Hill College, as children in grades 1–6 also moved to the Lincoln School District.

Residents continued to use the 1886 Cane Hill College building as a community center and later a visitor's center, which housed a small exhibit on Cane Hill's history, including that of the college. Today, the college building serves as the visual and social center of the community, as well as a visible reminder of its educational history and the role of the founding Cumberland Presbyterians.

ARCHAEOLOGY AT CANE HILL COLLEGE

While the 1886 Cane Hill College building still stands and can address questions regarding the use of landscape by the Cumberland Presbyterians who built it, the location of the 1850s college buildings and the 1868–1885 one, which was supposedly built at the same location, remained unclear. Documents provided only a vague reference to the location as being "on top of a limestone-faced hill from which a large spring flowed" (McCulloch 1989:7). The community is surrounded by hills and there are several springs. The surviving drawings show some of the surrounding landscape and indicate the buildings sat on a hill. But which hill? There are no aboveground structural ruins of any building that would have been large enough to serve as the college building. The local oral history has it that the 1850s and 1868 college buildings sat on the same hill as the surviving 1886 one, but on its crest. There is a large spring near this hill that supplied most of the town's water supply during the nineteenth century and into the twentieth. To determine whether this location could be the site of the former college, Historic Cane Hill turned to archaeological research. As much of Cane Hill's history and today's public exhibits center around the college, identifying its former location was important to Historic Cane Hill's public interpretations efforts. Finding its location was also vital to addressing research questions about how Cumberland Presbyterians utilized the landscape as a materialization of their religious ideology and how their landscape decisions helped unify the community.

In spring 2017 Historic Cane Hill purchased a thirteen-acre tract of land where Cane Hill College reportedly stood from the 1850s to 1885. Today, the partially wooded property sits on the hillcrest that overlooks Cane Hill, approximately 185 m southwest of the surviving 1886 building. On three sides, barbed wire fencing marks today's property boundaries. A grass-covered road, cleared in the 1980s, bisects the property north to south. To the west of this path, the terrain is relatively flat, while just to its south the elevation drops significantly toward the town. In May 2017 Historic Cane Hill funded an archaeological survey of two acres of the property with the main goal of determining whether it was indeed the former location of Cane Hill College. Crew members for the survey included four Auburn University at Montgomery students and three Cane Hill employees, with Bobby R. Braly, former executive director of Historic Cane Hill, and me serving as co-directors.

We began with a pedestrian survey of the site, recording visible artifacts or architectural features on the ground surface. Despite the thick ground cover and several fallen trees, crew members noted several brick fragments scattered throughout the property. The highest concentration could be seen in an approximately 50 × 30 m area, just to the north of the southern fence line and west of the grass road. Although no architectural features were noted, the abundance of brick fragments and their relatively large area of concentration highly suggested the former presence of a large, substantial brick structure. Additionally, the brick fragments indicated they were handmade, pointing to a pre-1900 construction date. While far from conclusive, the pedestrian survey provided enough evidence to suggest that the former Cane Hill College could have stood at this location.

For the next step of the project, we conducted a shovel-test survey of the property. We began by digging shovel-test pits (STPs) on 10-m centers. Based on the results from the first two rows of STPs, we closed the gap to 5-m intervals in order to better narrow down the site's boundaries. Overall, crew members dug eighty-one STPs, with only one negative for historic period artifacts. As observed with surface brick fragments, subsurface artifacts concentrated to the west of the modern grass, agricultural road, just north of the property's south boundary.

By far, architecture-related artifacts such as brick and mortar fragments, flat (window) glass, and nails outnumbered all other artifact types. Due to the substantial amount of brick fragments, we did not bag or count individual fragments, but they were the most-observed artifact. We recovered 434 cut nails and just over 1,000 fragments of flat glass. Container glass fragments were rare, with only 19 recovered. An additional 418 pieces of glass could not be positively identified as either container or flat glass, as they were melted and/or burned. Ceramics were also extremely rare, with only 16 sherds recovered. With the exception of one blue hand-painted whiteware sherd and one rim to a ginger beer bottle, all sherds were whiteware that lacked decoration. Other recovered artifacts included 12 pieces of slate, a clay marble found on the ground surface, a partial horseshoe, and a modern gun cartridge. Overall, the artifacts and their distribution across the site provide strong evidence that we located the former Cane Hill College.

Although architectural artifacts dominated the assemblage, they provide little information about the site's occupation date. The brick fragments indicate handmade bricks were used in construction while recovered nails were machine cut, both with production dates spanning the nineteenth century. Flat glass fragments, most likely from windows, provide the best opportunity for determining a more specific date range. Due to technological changes in production, window glass thickness steadily increased during the nineteenth century, providing archaeologists with a way to estimate its date of production. To account for regional differences in glass thickness and the varying rates at which it increased, archaeologists have developed multiple dating methods (Weiland 2009). Due to the mid to late nineteenth-century occupation date of the site and the region it is located in (Weiland 2009:30), I used Moir's (1983) and Schoen's (1990) methods. Additional justification for doing so came from Weiland's comparison of window glass dating methods, in which he concluded that the Moir and Schoen methods generally produced the best results (2009:39–40). For both methods, one measures the thickness of each glass fragment, and, with the use of a regression formula, an approximate date of production of the window glass is determined.

After removing flat glass fragments that were melted or otherwise damaged by heat, the thickness of the remaining 941 fragments was measured. The mean thickness was 2.05 mm, resulting in a Moir date of 1885.4 and a Schoen date of 1864. While these dates are a bit later than the documented construction of the college in the 1850s and its 1868 replacement, they are not unreasonable. However, the median measurement of 1.82 mm, with its Moir date of 1864.3 and Schoen date of 1847, provides much stronger evidence of construction in or around the 1850s.

The distribution of the architectural artifacts across the site provides stronger evidence of the site's past as College Hill College. The main campus building of the 1850s college is documented to have been a two-story 13.1 × 22.86 m (43 × 75 ft) brick structure. The widespread surface brick scatter does indicate that at least one brick structure, or at least a structure with brick foundations or piers, once stood here. While nearly every STP resulted in brick fragments, only a handful of them had intact bricks, large brick fragments, or mortar. STPs N105/E125 and N115/E145 had the only intact bricks. Whether they are foundations, piers, steps, or other architectural features is unknown at this time. Just east of N115/E145, three STPs had large brick fragments and chunks of mortar, suggesting intact brick features, or at least remnants of brick features, were nearby. Due to the distance between the STPs with intact brick, we are either looking at a single, large structure or at multiple buildings. Interestingly, the two STPs with intact brick line up roughly on a west-east axis, which may indicate a wall. Further excavations are needed to confirm that hypothesis; however, additional evidence does support a possible outline of a large structure.

We recovered the most architectural artifacts near the center of the grid, just west of the present-day grass path and north of the property's southern fence line (Figure 3.6). The size of this concentration is noteworthy, because at 25 × 25 m (82 × 82 ft) it approximates the reported 13.1 × 22.86 m (43 × 75 ft) dimensions of the 1850s main campus building and the later 1868 structure. In almost every STP located within this concentration, we also encountered a layer of architectural debris, primarily small brick and mortar fragments. The debris varied in depth from only a couple of centimeters up to 15 cm. In a more limited area (approximately 25 × 10 m), we encountered an ash layer. This layer also began 10–12 cm below the surface, and while the depth of the ash varied, it generally was only a couple of centimeters deep. Notably, in STPs with the ash layer, there was no architectural debris layer.

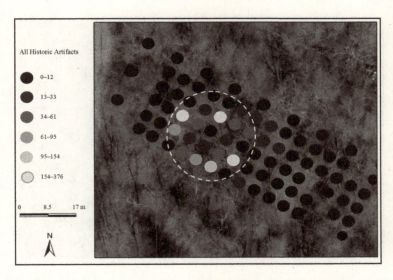

FIGURE 3.6. Distribution of all historic artifacts recovered from the survey, not including brick fragments and mortar. Area of highest artifact concentration is noted by the dashed circle. (Courtesy of Bobby R. Braly.)

Additionally, STPs with ash were much deeper than elsewhere on the site, often reaching 0.5–0.75 m before we encountered sterile subsoil or reached a depth where shovels would not work anymore. A possible explanation is that the area covered by the ash is the interior of a structure, with the depth of the STPs attributed to a cellar, basement, or, as seen with the extant 1886 college building, a crawl space, while the STPs with the architectural layer are closer to the former building's walls and foundations.

As noted, this area is also where the artifact density was greatest. The mean and median flat glass thickness measurements, 2.06 mm and 1.82 mm, respectively, were basically identical to those of the entire site (2.05 mm and 1.82 mm). Therefore, the Moir and Schoen dates indicate the former structure(s) at the site were likely constructed in the 1850s or so. After separating out the distributions of flat glass and nails, we found them to have similar concentration patterns with a noteworthy difference (Figures 3.7 and 3.8). The nails cluster in this area, but then drop off significantly, especially to the west and north. The flat glass also clusters here but is more widespread. Another noteworthy observation is the near void of glass toward the center of the concentration.

Does this distribution of nails and glass provide evidence of the outline of the 1858 main college building and the 1868 one, both of which measured

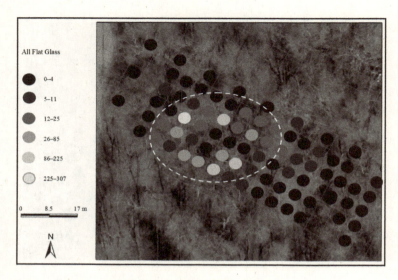

FIGURE 3.7. Distribution of all flat glass recovered from the survey. Area of highest concentration is noted by dashed oval. Note the near void of flat glass in the center of the oval. (Courtesy of Bobby R. Braly.)

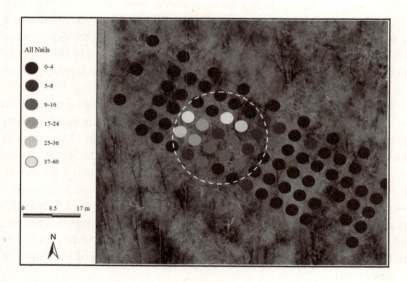

FIGURE 3.8. Distribution of all nails recovered from the survey. Area of highest concentration is noted by dashed circle. (Courtesy of Bobby R. Braly.)

13.1 × 22.86 m (43 × 75 ft)? Nails from floors and framing are expected to be found throughout the building's former footprint, while flat glass would likely be concentrated near the structure's exterior walls where windows would have been located. Additionally, the dimensions of this area are very close to those of the 1858 and 1868 structures. The distribution of nails and flat glass could also be confirmation that Union troops did destroy the 1850s college's main building with a single cannonball. Could the space void of flat glass actually be where the cannonball impacted and exploded, sending glass and nails outward? This scenario provides another explanation for why the flat glass was more widespread than the nails. Due to their weight, nails would not have flown as far as the glass. We do know that whether caused by a cannonball or some other means, Union troops did cause a fire that led to the destruction of Cane Hill College. Also, the 1868 college building burned in 1885, reportedly at the hands of an arsonist.

From the dimensions of the area of artifact concentration, the evidence of fire, and the brick scatter that indicate the former presence of a large, brick structure, the architectural artifacts strongly suggest Cane Hill College once stood on this site. This thinking is strengthened when we also consider the nonarchitectural artifacts.

First, the relative lack of such artifacts, especially ceramics (n=16) and container glass (n=18), is a strong indicator that the structure(s) identified were not residential in nature. Artifact assemblages from domestic sites are typically dominated by ceramic and container glass as such objects relate more to domestic activities, such as those involved in the preparation, cooking, serving, consumption, and storage of food and beverages. At public buildings, such as schools and churches, ceramic and glass objects are less common, as domestic activities rarely occur in them or the surrounding grounds. Instead, the artifact assemblages consist more of architectural artifacts, such as brick and mortar fragments, nails, and window glass.

Second, among the artifacts we recovered were 25 slate fragments. While slate is often considered architectural in nature since it was frequently used as a roofing material, these pieces were too thin to be associated with that purpose. However, during the nineteenth century and into the twentieth, many schools used slate for blackboards and students often had individual slate boards on which to write. Thus, a reasonable explanation for the presence of these thin, slate fragments is that they were fragments of slate blackboards that once hung in Cane Hill College's classrooms.

Third, although not a large sample, the ceramics do point to a mid to late nineteenth-century site occupation. As ceramic decorative styles changed frequently due to consumer taste and changes in technology and those preferences are documented in catalogs, business records, and other documents, ceramics typically provide very specific production dates. Fifteen of the 16 recovered ceramic sherds were whiteware, which was widely produced after 1830. One of them had blue hand-painting on it, which was popular from the 1830s through 1850s. The stoneware bottle rim is typical of ginger beer bottles that commonly date from the mid to late nineteenth century, although they were also produced before and after that time period (Greer 1981). The 18 container glass fragments, either amber or colorless, also suggest a mid to late nineteenth-century occupation of the site. Amber-colored glass first became commonly produced in the mid-nineteenth century, gained popularity throughout the remainder of the century, and continues to be manufactured today. Also, in the mid to late part of the nineteenth century, glass producers achieved a true colorless glass for the first time (Society for Historical Archaeology 2020). Although they comprise a small portion of the site's artifact assemblage, the ceramics and container glass narrow down the site's occupation to the mid to late nineteenth century. This date range corresponds to the 1850s–1862 Cane Hill College campus and the later 1868 college building.

Finally, in contrast to twenty-first-century cultural and social ideas of college life, the lack of artifacts related to tobacco and alcohol supports the idea that this site is indeed the Cumberland Presbyterian college. Beginning in the early nineteenth century, values associated with the Second Great Awakening spread rapidly, especially among Protestant denominations. Among the many changes to religious thinking was an emphasis placed on purity of the body, including the items a "good Christian" should, or should not, consume; this emphasis led to movements against the use of alcohol and tobacco. In 1851 the Cumberland Presbyterian General Assembly denounced alcohol use completely. In a resolution, they stated "that to make, buy, sell, or use as a beverage any spirituous or intoxicating liquors is an immorality; that it is not only unauthorized but forbidden by the word of God. We do, therefore, recommend to the several churches under our care, to abstain wholly from their use" (quoted in McDonnold 1888:613–614). While they did not issue a full denunciation of the use of tobacco, four years later the General Assembly proclaimed that "the use of tobacco, by chewing and smoking, is unnecessary" (quoted in Barrus et al. 1972:254).

As Cane Hill College was a Cumberland Presbyterian school, students and professors were not allowed to use alcohol and the trustees banned their use of tobacco, at least on college grounds (Cane Hill College 1877:12). Additionally, President Earle was a strong proponent of prohibition and was a leader of the temperance movement in the state (Basham 1969:170). During our survey, crew members did not recover a single tobacco pipe bowl or stem, or any other evidence of tobacco usage. Additionally, evidence related to the use of alcohol is extremely limited. The only possible direct evidence of alcohol use is the single ginger beer bottle sherd. However, even that evidence is not overwhelming, as many ginger beer bottles at the time actually contained nonalcoholic beverages. Container glass was also rare throughout the site, with only 18 glass fragments recovered, and it remains unknown whether they held alcohol, medicine, or any number of other possible nonalcoholic liquids.

Based on this evidence, there is little doubt that this site does indeed represent the 1850s Cane Hill College campus destroyed during the Civil War and the subsequent building that replaced it in 1868 and later burned in 1885. With strong confidence in the college's specific location, it is now possible to turn attention to how Cane Hill's Cumberland Presbyterians used landscape to their benefit and how by doing so, they ultimately shaped the Cane Hill community.

CANE HILL COLLEGE'S USE OF THE LANDSCAPE

Today's town of Cane Hill is located in a valley formed by Jordan Creek, generally on a north-south orientation. Ridges overlook the community from both the west and the east. Throughout its history, Cane Hill's businesses, public buildings, and most of its residences have largely been situated along a road, today's Arkansas Highway 45, which runs just west of Jordan Creek. However, the Cumberland Presbyterians did not place their structures in the center of the town, rather situating their churches and schools on the western ridge overlooking the community.

Although the secondary sources vary in detail concerning the date of the town's earliest Cumberland Presbyterian joint church and school building, referred to as the "meeting house by early settlers," they do agree that it sat on a hill. Both Carnahan (1954:8) and Miller and Williams (1969:8) state that the first church also served as a school and that it stood where the town later established Cane Hill Cemetery. McCulloch also refers to this location, writing that in 1832 or 1833, the Cumberland Presbyterian congregation constructed a new church, "located on the grounds of the present Cane Hill Cemetery" (1989:2). The cemetery is located on the western hillside toward the northern end of the town limits. Today there is no visible evidence of their first meeting house, or any other building, meaning that the local lore remains unconfirmed. In reference to the early 1830s Cumberland Presbyterian school, Richardson (1955:55) states that it sat "on a hill near the village." While the exact location of this school remains unknown, the secondary sources agree the meeting house overlooked the community from a nearby hillside.

As already mentioned, the Cumberland Presbyterians constructed a new building for their school as it evolved into the Cane Hill Collegiate Institute in the early 1850s. Again, secondary sources are vague as to the campus's exact location. Local residents, many of whom are descendants from the founding Cumberland Presbyterian families, state that the 1850s campus and the 1868 college building sat on the crest of the western ridge that overlooks the community, which is supported by archaeological research. When fire destroyed their 1868 college building, Cumberland Presbyterians constructed another one. While it is located on the same ridge as the previous two, it is located about halfway up the hill rather than on its crest. Why they did not rebuild on the same site is unknown. Despite its location, the Cane Hill College building still dominates the Cane Hill landscape.

It is not unusual for religious or government buildings to be placed on hilltops. Being so constructed, they are often the most visually prominent structure on the landscape, a placement that implies their important role within the society, not only to members of the society but to visitors as well. As already discussed in the context of St. Luke's, a hilltop location coupled with the overall height of the structure places religious buildings closer to the heavens and therefore, to the god(s). In Puritan New England, the hilltop location of churches related to the Puritan belief that they were a "City upon a Hill." Puritan leader John Winthrop introduced this idea in 1630 as he delivered a sermon onboard a ship as he traveled from England to settle in Massachusetts, stating, "For we must consider that we shall be as a city upon a hill. The eyes of all people are upon us" (Winthrop 1630). The Puritans saw themselves and their new settlement as a role model, with God, represented through the church, at being the center of their community.

Several archaeologists have examined other reasons for the placement of religious and public buildings on hilltops. As part of his extensive archaeological research in Annapolis, Maryland, Leone (2005) examined the planned landscape of the colonial city. While his study is primarily an "examination of the structure of power based on changing wealth" (Leone 2005:31), which is not the focus of this study, his description of colonial Annapolis is helpful here. Designed by Francis Nicholson, Maryland's royal governor from 1694 to 1698, Annapolis's town plan placed both the Maryland State House and St. Anne's Church—which represented the established Church of England—as prominent features of the landscape. Following Baroque urban design, Nicholson utilized lines of sight to direct people's eyes to Annapolis's two most important buildings. While he designed many of the landscape features that created these lines of sight, including the circles that the two buildings sit on, Nicholson also took advantage of Annapolis's natural landscape features, in particular hills (Leone 2005:8–9). Besides leading to both buildings being very visible, Leone also examines how their hilltop location helped express the natural order of the state government's power. Based on ideas presented by Bentham (1962) and Foucault (1979), Leone interprets the windowed dome of the State House as a panopticon that overlooks the city, and its citizens, from its hilltop location. While Annapolis's citizens could watch over their government, their government could also watch them. This mutual surveillance helped promote social order, citizenship, and the new nation (Leone 2005:96–100).

The idea of a panopticon also emerges in a study by Lydon (2009) of Ebenezer, a nineteenth-century Moravian mission located in Victoria, Australia. Through her research, Lydon shows how Moravians used the natural landscape to announce their presence in colonial Australia and to impose their religious ideology, social order, and paternalistic ideas on the Aborigines they housed and who lived in the surrounding area. One significant way they did this was to by constructing their church, mission house, school, and dormitories—all of which represented Moravian values and beliefs—along a ridge top that overlooked mission lands. Lydon stressed how this location provided Moravian missionaries with a panoptic view from their ridge-top buildings, allowing them to observe the Aborigines as they labored in the fields, as well as their activities in the residential areas (Lydon 2009:115). Furthermore, the hilltop location led to these buildings being the most prominent structures on the surrounding landscape, announcing the Moravian (and English) presence and power in the colony (Lydon 2009:110).

Similarly, from its hilltop location on the western edge of the village, Cane Hill College had a panoptic view looking over the town and its people. Importantly, surveillance of the population's behavior fit within the self-understood mandate of the Cumberland Presbyterians, who had strict rules about how godly people should behave. Session minutes from both the Cane Hill and Salem congregations mention several instances of members being accused of drunkenness, swearing, dancing, and other unspecific forms of "immoral" or "unchristian" conduct (Lemke 1955; Session Minutes of Salem Congregation of the Cumberland Presbyterian Church, Boonsboro, 1865–1905, Washington County Historical Society, University of Arkansas Special Collections Library, MS C9128). Through the Civil War, the Salem congregation did not have a separate church and used their college's chapel as its place of worship (Richardson 1955:51). The Cane

Hill congregation did have a separate church building, referred to as the "White Church," but it was located a few miles north of the settlement. Therefore, while it was not a church building per se, the college was the one visible representation of the Cumberland Presbyterian Church and its values within the geographic limits of the community. Residents who belonged to either of the Cumberland Presbyterian congregations, and even those who did not, may have felt that the Church was watching over their actions from above.

The panopticon interpretation for the hilltop placement of Cane Hill College has its merits. However, given the historical context of Cane Hill and the Cumberland Presbyterian Church, especially its emphasis on education, there is another explanation reflecting DeMarrais et al.'s "materialization of ideology" (1996). Although the Cane Hill community was not designed in the Baroque style as seen in colonial Annapolis, the Cumberland Presbyterians took advantage of lines of sight, in particular, with their use of the hilltop that overlooked the town. Everyone in Cane Hill—area residents, visitors, members of the Cumberland Presbyterian Church, or members of other local churches—would have seen the college sitting high on the hill. As DeMarrais et al. state, public monuments, including large buildings such as the college, "associate a group with a place and represent the power and authority of its leaders" (1996:18). Not only did Cumberland Presbyterians first establish the Cane Hill community, several of its first settlers were directly involved with the creation of the Cumberland Presbyterian Church in Kentucky and Tennessee. By placing Cane Hill College and their earlier schools on hilltops, Cumberland Presbyterian leadership guaranteed their buildings were the most visible structures on the landscape. What better way to showcase their "power and authority?"

But why would Cumberland Presbyterians choose to highlight school buildings on the hilltop that directly overlooked Cane Hill rather than their churches? Although the Salem congregation used the building for church services, the college was first and foremost a place for higher education. It was not a church that also held college classes. It was a college that also served as a place of worship. To address that question, it is important to recall the emphasis Cumberland Presbyterians placed on education, especially for men interested in joining the ministry. It is also important to recall that one of the reasons Cumberland Presbyterians split from the Presbyterian Church is that the latter mandated that its ministers be "classically" educated.

But education was not just reserved for the ministers. Cumberland Presbyterians believed that education was vital for *all* its members, including women. For the Church, religion and education went hand in hand. Church leaders felt an obligation to educate laypeople in order to improve society (Gage 2006:47). In 1855, shortly after Cane Hill College was chartered, the General Assembly of the Cumberland Presbyterian Church stated, "No church can accomplish the ends of its creation without the correlative influence of education" (Minutes of the General Assembly 1855:55, quoted in Barrus et al. 1972:215). To assist with providing their laity an education, the Cumberlands founded a number of institutions of higher education, primarily in frontier areas (Barrus et al. 1972:227). In 1835, shortly after the Cumberland Presbyterians created their first school in Cane Hill, the school's Professor Samuel Doak Lowry said, "We owe it to ourselves and to God to kindle a light *on this hilltop* [emphasis added] which will over-top all surrounding hills and mountains, and bear intelligence and lights and gladness on the wrings of its beans far off to distant regions." (Lowry, June 23, 1835, quoted in Gage 2006:47).

By placing Cane Hill School, Cane Hill Collegiate Institute, and Cane Hill College on the hilltop overlooking the village, Cumberland Presbyterians deliberately used the natural landscape to make their places of higher education the most visible buildings in the community. By doing so, they materially expressed their emphasis and commitment to education within their religious identity. Additionally, it was a way to show the Presbyterian Church that they did indeed take education seriously. Cumberland Presbyterian ministers could, and often did, have a "classical" education, even in more remote locations such as Cane Hill. It was also their way of justifying themselves and their split from the Presbyterian Church. It did not hurt that, as already mentioned, the location—with its panoptic view of the town—allowed Cumberland Presbyterians to express their local power and authority and reinforce its values within the context of their immediate geographic vicinity. Despite the presence of other churches, such as the Methodist Episcopal Church, for all intents and purposes Cane Hill was a Cumberland Presbyterian community.

For most of its existence, Cane Hill's created landscape has focused on Cane Hill College, whether at its former location at the crest of the hill overlooking the town or its current location halfway up that same hill. From the town's inception, Cane Hill's community identity formed and revolved around the Cumberland Presbyterians' emphasis on religion and education. Throughout the mid-nineteenth century, the various college buildings and its hilltop campus aided in maintaining and strengthening the Cumberland Presbyterian identity, while also spreading that identity and values to the member of the larger community. When the college trustees constructed the extant 1886 college building, they had no idea of the impact that building would have on the people of Cane Hill and the community itself for generations to come. As the town's influence and population declined, especially after Cane Hill School closed in the early half of the twentieth century, their building continued to materially express the role of education in the community. Even after its days as an educational institution ended, the former college building continued to help shape and maintain Cane Hill's identity, and, today, it remains the "heart" of the community.

CHAPTER FOUR

Forming Communities and Identities

> Whether intended or not, architecture and designed landscapes serve as grand mnemonic devices that record and transmit vital aspects of culture and history.
>
> —Marc Treib, introduction, *Spatial Recall* (2009:xii)

As NEW SETTLEMENTS developed in the United States, the construction of churches and other places of worship was typically not a top priority. Instead, shelter, agricultural pursuits, defense, and commercial endeavors took precedence. As seen in St. Paul's Parish, Cahaba, and Cane Hill, in young settlements it often took one to two decades for religious structures to appear on the landscape. However, that does not mean religion was unimportant to residents. Early settlers would continue their religious practices and uphold their beliefs in their private homes and/or meet with fellow worshippers at residences or public buildings to worship together despite the absence of a dedicated religious edifice.

Nevertheless, the construction of a religious structure was a significant turning point for any growing community—whether a geographic community or a community of worshippers—as it symbolized the progress it had already made, its present stability, and a commitment to its future (Lane 2012:251–252). In many communities' early years, physical religious structures represented the unity of the members of a particular religious organization, as well as the cohesiveness of the larger community as a whole (Lane 2012:256). How this solidarity played out varied between communities. In early colonial South Carolina, the Church of England had the power and financial backing of the proprietary government since it was the established religion of the colony. However, in St. Paul's Parish, Dissenters far outnumbered Anglicans. Rather than working against one another, they worked together, or in this case, worshipped together, with many of the parish's Dissenters attending services at St. Paul's Parish Church. Meanwhile, in the early decades of Cahaba, no one denomination had political authority over another and there were no significant differences in their number of worshippers. Instead, the town's various religious organizations worked together to construct a shared structure, the Union Church, and established a rotating schedule of worship services. Only later did they have the congregations, funds, and other means to support their own individual places of worship. In Cane Hill, Cumberland Presbyterians founded the settlement and, therefore, held religious, political, economic, and social power. Other denominations were present, such as the Methodists; however, their individual congregations and religious structures did not have the presence or influence that the Cumberland Presbyterians enjoyed.

One aspect of DeMarrais et al.'s "materialization of ideology" concept is that public monuments and landscapes aid in the development and maintenance of group unity and cohesion. In each of the three case studies presented, the landscape and architecture decisions made by religious leaders united groups of people from different backgrounds, ultimately forming new communities with shared common cultural identifiers. In St. Paul's Parish and Cahaba, race—and its related socioeconomic status—was the primary cultural identifier. Meanwhile, in Cane Hill, the founding Cumberland Presbyterians' identity, especially their religious beliefs and focus on education, spread throughout the larger community. Later as the town declined, the survival of Cane Hill itself became a central consideration and community identity shifted to focus on the town's heritage and its Cumberland Presbyterian history.

St. Paul's Parish Church, St. Luke's Episcopal Church, and Cane Hill College were all designed, constructed, and used by dominant groups of various communities. Leaders of each religious organization made conscious decisions regarding the architectural style and overall design of their buildings, as well as how to utilize the natural and cultural landscapes they sat upon. They based their choices partially on their religious ideologies. Consequently, each building was a "materialization of the ideology" of each respective organization. However, other factors also played into their decision-making. As DeMarrais et al. (1996) state, in the past, dominant groups also used public monuments, such as religious structures and landscapes, to send messages regarding their power and claim to the land both to members of their own group and to members of the less dominant groups. They also unified people and promoted group solidarity. Each of these three case studies provides examples of how religious organizations purposely used architecture and landscape as material expressions of their religious *and* social ideologies, and of their power, influence, and goals. As a result, their religious buildings symbolized not only their religious background but also how dominant members of the community identified themselves ethnically, racially, and socially. The intentional decisions of religious leaders to use landscape and architecture to their benefit had consequences that they likely never intended.

ST. PAUL'S PARISH

This book began with the early eighteenth-century Church of England, or Anglican Church, in early colonial South Carolina. Leaders of St. Paul's Parish Church purposely used both landscape and architecture as material expressions of their religious and social ideologies and goals. Through the positioning of Anglican churches on the colonial landscape, they developed the cultural landscape to their benefit. They situated their churches in strategic landscape locations to make them as conspicuous as possible to travelers along the Stono River, even breaking Church of England canon law when necessary to achieve that goal. St. Paul's Parish leaders were not the only ones to do so. A regional analysis of South Carolina's other early eighteenth-century Anglican churches indicates that several of them were also placed on the landscape to be highly visible from the riverways they sat along, even if that meant deviating from the east-west canonical axis.

Anglican officials saw their churches as physical manifestations of the presence and power of the Church of England over the various dissenting religious groups, which would have been important to them after years of fighting for establishment. Additionally, the prominence of English churches on the Carolina landscape signified English control of the land and over all its people. By materializing the Anglican Church's and the English's colonial presence and power on the Carolina landscape, church leaders, many of whom also held political roles, were able to legitimize, bolster, and transmit their ideologies, beliefs, and cultural practices (DeMarrais et al. 1996:17). By doing so, they strengthened ties among Anglicans and English settlers in the colony, while also drawing in Dissenters and non-English people to the Anglican Church, and promoting a greater acceptance of the English proprietary government.

While landscape decisions played a role in unifying the white population, at least in St. Paul's Parish, architectural decisions also played a role in that process. A combination of archaeological and documentary evidence and the study of extant early eighteenth-century Anglican churches demonstrates that St. Paul's Parish Church most likely had a plain, simple design. This Low Church style was likely an intentional decision of St. Paul's church supervisors, Seabrook, Hicks, and Farr, in order to materially express the religious diversity in a parish where the majority of white settlers were Dissenters, in particular, Presbyterians. It was likely also an attempt to attract Dissenters to St. Paul's.

Whether they were drawn to the Anglican Church through landscape, architecture, or other means, why would Dissenters make the conscious decision to attend an Anglican church? What did they gain from doing so? How could they identify with the Church itself, along with other parishioners? How did their attendance at Anglican churches help unify the white population? Here I explore answers to those questions, ultimately concluding that by attracting Dissenters to their church, church leaders paved the way for a shift in identity among the colony's white settlers—from one based largely on religion (Anglican or Dissenter) to one based primarily on skin color (white or Black). My discussion for St. Paul's Parish and its church centers on white settlers and parishioners as they were the ones who interacted within the church on a regular basis. During most of the eighteenth century, and especially during its first half, enslaved peoples, whether Black or Indigenous, had little interaction within church buildings themselves. While they likely played a large role in the construction of churches and their maintenance afterwards, they were rarely allowed to worship inside of them, or even hear Christian teachings from the SPG missionaries.

Due to the Carolina colony's stance on religious tolerance, dissenting religious groups were welcome to worship freely and to construct their own churches. However, for whatever reasons, many Dissenters still choose to attend Anglican churches. One possible reason is that in an environment with few dissenting churches, Dissenters may have thought joining an Anglican Church service was better than not attending one at all. Another explanation is that Dissenters benefited socially, economically, and politically from their attendance at St. Paul's and other Anglican churches. Especially for those seeking political advancement, aligning oneself with the official religion of the colony held advantages. Through their presence at their local Anglican church, Dissenters showed support of the established church. Additionally, attendance gave them the opportunity to discuss political events with their fellow parishioners who were responsible for electing men to the General

Assembly and other political positions. The desire for political gain provides an explanation for why Landgrave Bellinger, a devout Dissenter, donated several acres of land to be used as the location of St. Paul's Parish Church, cemetery, and glebe lands (Bolton 1982:24; Conveyance from Estate of Landgrave Bellinger, 1706, Records of St. Paul's, Stono, 1706–1864 (0273.03.32), South Carolina Historical Society, Charleston). As a landgrave, Bellinger held a high political position in the government and had ambitions to become the colony's governor. He would have likely gained support of Anglicans through his donation.

Dissenting groups also realized the benefits of allying themselves with the Church of England. In the early 1700s, as the Church gained political power, the colony's French Huguenot population recognized the benefits of affiliating themselves with the Anglican Church, in particular the High Anglicans (Bolton 1971:67). In exchange for their votes in support of establishment, the South Carolina Anglican Church provided Huguenots with their own parish, St. Denis, located within the boundaries of St. Thomas Parish. At St. Denis, Huguenots used a French translation of the Book of Common Prayer and held services in French. Although they sacrificed some of their Calvinist practices by joining the Church of England, Huguenots maintained some of their cultural practices, while also gaining political power as a group (Bolton 1982:26; Linder 2000:33). Individual French Huguenots also gained politically as they received support from Anglicans in parish elections.

Attending an Anglican church also provided a sense of "home" to English settlers, whether Anglican or Dissenter. Although early settlers to South Carolina had come from across Europe (Joseph and Zierden 2002:1), the vast majority were English, having arrived directly from England or through Barbados. Especially for newly arrived settlers, South Carolina was unlike anything they had seen back home. The environment and landscape were completely foreign to them. Early colonists had to learn to navigate tidal waters, experiment with different crops they never had grown before, and contend with alligators and other types of strange animals. People familiar with the village or urban lifestyles of England now found themselves living several miles from their nearest neighbors and at least a day's trip into town. The semitropical climate posed new problems as well, especially the hot, humid conditions and the "fevers" it brought during the late summers. Additionally, a majority of the people living in the colony looked and sounded different from the English colonists. In addition to the non-English European settlers, prior to 1717 many American Indians still held their lands there, and within a few decades, tens of thousands of enslaved West Africans were brought into the colony. Even for a Dissenter, walking into an Anglican church and being surrounded by English practices, traditions, and people who wore familiar clothing and spoke a familiar language must have provided a sense of home. It was a way to maintain and express their English, or even European, identity, and in some way made their adjustment to their new home easier (Hawkins 1983; Linder 2000; Woolverton 1984).

But why the need for unity among South Carolina's white settlers? One possible answer lies in the increasingly diverse makeup of the colony's population. For the first time in many of their lives, white settlers found themselves in the minority of the population. With significant events such as the 1715 Yamasee War and, later, the 1739 Stono Rebellion, they soon realized that the religious differences between Anglicans and the various dissenting groups were not nearly as important as their fear of neighboring American Indians and of the increasing majority of enslaved Africans. Overcoming their religious differences and focusing on threats, both real and perceived, from the Indigenous and Black populations became a priority. Whether one was Anglican, Dissenter, English, French, German, or from elsewhere in Europe became less important over time. Instead, whether one was white or nonwhite became a central issue. As seen elsewhere in South Carolina (Zierden 2002) and in other colonies in the eighteenth century (Epperson 1990; Silver 2008), white settlers set aside their religious differences and focused on what they did share, namely a common European background and, subsequently, a common skin color.

The development of a unified white community was especially important in St. Paul's Parish as it was on the southern outskirts of the colony and included some of the closest European American settlement to Indian lands, as well as to lands claimed by the Spanish. By 1720 the Indigenous and Spanish threats to South Carolina had dissipated, but the African population continued to grow exponentially. At that time, enslaved Africans comprised an estimated 60 to 69 percent of the overall population of St. Paul's Parish (Morgan 1998:96). As the Black majority in St. Paul's continued to rise to 80 to 89 percent by 1760 (Morgan 1998:97), the church became one of the few places in the parish where white settlers could be among others whom they could identify with more ethnically and racially. This would have been especially true during the first half of the eighteenth century, as white enslavers rarely allowed their enslaved laborers to attend worship services, or even learn about Christianity, out of concern that if they converted, they could no longer be enslaved.

Whatever their reasons, notable numbers of Dissenters chose to attend services at St. Paul's Parish Church and other Anglican churches within the colony. As a result, the South Carolina Anglican Church and its individual parish churches served as unifying forces in the relatively young colony. Anglican churches provided common places for white settlers, both Anglicans and Dissenters, to congregate together in worship but also to socialize, conduct business, push political agendas, and to feel more "English." Especially in the colony's more remote frontier parishes where white settlement was still widely scattered, Anglican churches became the "heart" of the parish community for both Anglicans and Dissenters. They were places where white settlers worshipped side-by-side, mitigating their various religious, cultural, or ethnic differences. Ultimately, South Carolina's European American population, which once identified themselves as Anglican or Dissenters, began to identify themselves by their white skin color, distinguishing them from the darker skin of their enslaved Africans and of Indigenous peoples, both freed and enslaved. Consequently, they constructed a new identity for the white South Carolina community, one that led to skin color being the primary attribute that defined white identity rather than religious beliefs. As a consequence, they reinforced what it meant to be white (and thus Black) and further strengthened the racial differences between the two. This shift in identity led to a further strengthening of South Carolina's developing plantation economy, its growing dependence on enslaved Africans, and the colony's growing racial divide.

CAHABA

After the end of the Revolutionary War, the Anglican Church in the newly created United States of America formally severed its ties with the Church of England and formed the Protestant Episcopal Church. Despite this formal separation, the two organizations maintained similar religious beliefs, practices, ideologies, and doctrine, as well as similar ways of materially expressing them. Therefore, during the early decades of the nineteenth century, as the Church of England began to shift their Low Church ideologies to more High Church ones, so did the Episcopal Church.

The Gothic Revival architecture of St. Luke's Episcopal Church demonstrates how ideological changes between the eighteenth-century Low Church ideologies and those of the mid-nineteenth-century High Church were expressed through material culture. Its design also reflected the social status and ideologies of its more affluent, white congregation members and their beliefs regarding slavery and the segregation of enslaved, Black parishioners. The more opulent and elaborate nature of St. Luke's may have also made a statement to other churches in town. Gundersen has noted that, especially in towns still in their early development, competition often arose between different denominations as they constructed their individual churches after initially sharing a single structure (1987:266). As Cahaba's various denominations started building their own individual churches and moved out of the shared Union Church, it is plausible that a friendly competition arose. Having the "best church" may have been a matter of pride, but it also could have attracted new parishioners to one's church. Therefore, the more opulent nature of St. Luke's may have been driven by the Episcopalians wanting to best their neighbors. Furthermore, its prominent location at the center of the town and along the bank of the Alabama River, plus its 27.43 m (90 ft) tall spire made it the most visible structure in Cahaba and sent messages regarding its presence, influence, and power to townspeople, visitors, and passersby. Its visual prominence and design also showcased Cahaba as a modern, cosmopolitan town.

While wealth and background comprised parts of the community identity of many parishioners, so did race. Unlike in St. Paul's Parish, where architectural decisions made by parish leaders to intentionally attract Dissenters to their church unintentionally led to white settlers restructuring their identity to center on race, in Cahaba, architectural decisions were purposely made to reinforce and strengthen notions of race that were already firmly entrenched in society. The primary way St. Luke's architecture upheld white racial ideology was the creation of architecturally distinct spaces with the construction of its gallery and separate entrance for its Black parishioners. Decisions to add these separated spaces reinforced and united white Episcopalians behind their white identity. Likewise, and most likely unintentionally, it did the same for the Black community. I return to this point shortly.

By using architecture to reflect racial, social, and economic identities and ideas, St. Luke's created a place where white parishioners could gather and socialize with others who shared in their common racial, social, and economic backgrounds. It was also a place where people who desired to identify with those backgrounds could congregate. By attending services at St. Luke's, one could give the appearance of being wealthier or more cosmopolitan by associating with people who did have those backgrounds. Not unlike the Dissenters who attended services at Anglican churches in early colonial South Carolina, there would have been social, economic, and possibly political advantages to individuals who joined the Episcopalian church, which was known to have some of the wealthiest and most influential citizens among its congregation.

Ultimately, this shared identity among St. Luke's white community, and that of the larger Cahaba community, was not strong enough to survive the effects and aftermath of the Civil War. Cahaba faced several hardships—loss of their railroad, devastating floods, and of course, loss of family and community members. But ultimately, it was the emancipation of the enslaved labor force that caused the most upheaval to their way of life. For many white people, emancipation caused them to lose parts of their identity. They were no longer owners of enslaved people. They were no longer wealthy. They were no longer planters due to the loss of their labor source to cultivate their land. However, they could still identify themselves as white. Although beyond the scope of this book, the loss of several aspects of white identity and fear of losing their power to a majority of now freed Black people ultimately led to the Jim Crow Laws and segregation, the rise of the Ku Klux Klan, race riots, and racially motivated murders and other violence throughout the twentieth century and into the twenty-first century.

While Cahaba's white population fragmented in the years during and after the Civil War, the newly emancipated Black community persisted and even thrived, at least for a few years. In the years immediately following the end of the Civil War and emancipation, Cahaba became an African American community, known for being a place where Black politicians made strides in gaining and maintaining political power in the early days of Reconstruction. Cahaba gained such a reputation for Black politicians that it was often referred to as the "Mecca of the Radical Republican party" (Derry 1997:19). In addition to being a safe harbor for Black politicians, Cahaba also became an early center of the African Methodist Episcopal (AME) church in the state. Cahaba's Black community organized St. Paul's AME Church and moved into the former St. Paul's Methodist Church. Additionally, a school for the children of Black tenant farmers formed in the lot adjoining St. Paul's AME Church. Although no longer used for educational pursuits after 1952, the former school building still stands next to the ruins of St. Paul's AME Church, which burned in 1954 (Figure 4.1).

The persistence of Cahaba's freed Black community is reminiscent of Morris's (2017) discussion of "homeplace," specifically her own family's homeplace. Borrowing ideas from bell hooks (1990), Morris describes homeplaces as places where "Black farmsteaders created meaningful lives for themselves in a society structured in racialized inequality" (2017:29). They were places where people supported each other, whether they were part of the same family or of a larger community (2017:37). Morris also describes what she sees as "persistence through land ownership and occupation and cultivation of a safe, private decolonized space as a quintessential site of resistance for free African Americans in the 19th century" (2017:30).

While it was not technically a homeplace, I see parallels with St. Luke's Episcopal Church and Cahaba. In a sense, St. Luke's was a homeplace that provided a place for its community of Black parishioners to resist the messages of control expressed by its white leaders and ultimately to persist.

FIGURE 4.1. Early to mid-twentieth-century school that children of Black tenant farmers living in and near Cahaba attended. (Photograph by Kimberly Pyszka.)

Therefore, I argue that at least part of the reason for the growth and persistence of Cahaba's Black community after the Civil War may be traced back to the architecturally distinct spaces of St. Luke's. Although such features were intended as a show of power and control by the white community to reinforce their racial and social identities, they also unintentionally helped Black parishioners shape and reinforce their own identity. These distinct spaces provided a homeplace where Black parishioners could gather and socialize with others who shared in their common racial, social, and economic backgrounds. Through their interactions while sharing the space of St. Luke's gallery, Black parishioners created nonfamily connections. They met and socialized with other members of Cahaba's Black community, including those from outlaying plantations. Through their shared experiences of slavery, segregation, and other forms of racism, a new Black community arose, one whose members had a say in and control over.

CANE HILL

In South Carolina and Alabama, race became a major factor in the identity of the dominant groups, likely due to the large amounts of labor needed for Carolina's rice fields, Alabama's cotton fields, and their respective plantation economies. Arkansas was also a slave state and many of the Cumberland Presbyterian leaders and congregation members were enslavers. However, race and racial identity do not appear to be as important in the Cane Hill community, at least on the surface. Other factors shaped a large part of the Cane Hill's community identity, but racial differences did exist. Many of Cane Hill's residents, including leaders and members of the Cumberland Presbyterian Church, owned enslaved peoples and fought for the Confederacy. Enslaved African Americans labored in the surrounding agricultural fields, orchards, and mills, and while not documented, their labor very likely constructed most of the town's residences, churches, and public buildings, including those related to Cane Hill College.

Still, rather than race, Cane Hill's nineteenth-century community identity primarily centered on religion, education, milling, and agriculture. First and foremost were religion and education. Cane Hill's early founders, many of whom were also Cumberland Presbyterian leaders, envisioned a place of higher education to train men for the ministry and to fulfill the Cumberland Presbyterian focus on education for all. These leaders expressed this commitment through their educational buildings, in particular their landscape decisions to situate the various Cane Hill College buildings on the hillside overlooking the community. For anyone who lived, worked, or visited Cane Hill, the presence of Cumberland Presbyterian religious and educational structures overlooking the town reinforced the important role of religion and education in the community. These observers also likely acknowledged the role of the Cumberland Presbyterian Church and its college in the growth of their community—not just demographically but also religiously, educationally, socially, and even economically. The local Methodist church and congregation recognized the importance of the college and the need for it to survive, as witnessed when they opened their doors to students after fire destroyed the 1868 college building (Basham 1969:152; Campbell 1985:49). Finally, the hilltop location also led to the buildings having a panopticon view of the town and its residents, reminding all, whether Cumberland Presbyterian or not, of the presence, power, and strict values of the Cumberland Presbyterian Church.

With Cane Hill College's closure in 1891, the building converted to the community's K–12 public school. No longer affiliated with the Cumberland Presbyterian Church, or any other religious institution, the former college building remained a material representation of the value of education. Not only did most of the area's children gain an education in the building but as is common in many small towns, the community's social activities revolved around the school building and its grounds. From sporting events to theater productions, from picnics to agricultural activities, most of Cane Hill's identity continued to be centered on Cane Hill School (Braly 2019).

Even after the school's doors closed for the last time in the early 1950s, the former Cane Hill College has continued to be the visual and social center of the town. It also remains a materialization of community ideology and continues to develop and maintain group identity, but one that now centers on its history and heritage. By the late twentieth century, the community's identity had shifted to remembering and protecting its history, specifically the history and contributions of the Cumberland Presbyterian Church and of Cane Hill College. Beginning in the 1980s, a group of area residents, many of whom are descendants of the original settlers, volunteered to maintain the former college building and preserve its history. They inventoried documents and photographs related to Cane Hill, in particular the college. Inside the former college building, they developed a small museum exhibit to display its history and inform visitors of the town's past. To aid with the continued care and maintenance of the college building, in the early 2000s several local people formed the Cane Hill College Association, a 501(3) nonprofit organization (Braly 2020). With the founding of Historic Cane Hill Inc. in 2013, preservation efforts spread throughout the town and into the larger western Washington County community. However, the former college building remained the primary focus of these efforts, culminating with its $1.4 million renovation and May 2017 grand reopening (Braly 2019).

In many ways, the former Cane Hill College building has contributed to the very survival of Cane Hill and its community. Once a bustling nineteenth-century town, by the later part of the twentieth century its population had declined drastically as many younger people moved to seek greater employment, educational, and social opportunities elsewhere. At present, only fifty or so residents live within the community's geographic boundaries. However, today's Cane Hill community extends well beyond the geographic boundaries of the small town to include descendants of the founding families, the school's former students and their descendants, and people involved with historic preservation efforts. Additionally, as more guests visit Cane Hill to tour its new museum and renovated buildings, walk its nature trails, attend a meeting or conference, or even get married, new community members are continually being added. For all, the Cumberland Presbyterian's restored 1886 Cane Hill College building represents the community's new identity, one that is proud of its history and heritage and is dedicated to historic preservation efforts, while also continuing to strengthen old bonds and create new ones.

From the early colonial period in South Carolina to antebellum Central Alabama to mid to late nineteenth-century Northwest Arkansas, religious landscapes and buildings have played a large role in shaping the culture of the southeastern United States. Religious organizations have expressed their identity through their architectural and landscape design choices, leading to the formation of new community identities in the eighteenth and nineteenth centuries. Those identities have since evolved into the Southeastern identities of the twenty-first century.

Religious identity remains a key aspect of the Southeast's culture. For many Southeasterners, it is the primary way they identify themselves. The region has even earned the nickname, the "Bible Belt," due to the high percentage of people who identify themselves as religious and because of the role religious beliefs play in local politics and society as a whole. At the same time, as seen in St. Paul's Parish and St. Luke's in Cahaba, Southeastern identities developed around racial identity, just as much, if not more so, then religious identity. While great strides have been made in the past several decades, the effects of slavery and segregation—namely, continued injustice and unequal access to health care, education, and job opportunities—are still very much a part of life today in the Southeast. While other factors contributed to the development of identity in today's Southeast, the seemingly innocent architectural choices religious leaders intentionally made regarding their religious buildings, and their use of the landscape to showcase them, must be a consideration.

Epilogue

Today's Religious Landscapes

> Religious spaces have a kind of agency. They are man-made products that have an impact on human experience. Concretely, buildings limit or direct movement, impress visitors, affect the senses, evoke connotations. Neither an empty cipher with no intrinsic meaning whatsoever nor an authoritative text, a building provides opportunities for processes of identification within a particular social context.
>
> —Oskar Verkaaik, in *Religious Architecture: Anthropological Perspectives* (2013:12)

As an anthropological archaeologist, my research centers on past religious landscapes; however, I also recognize that religious landscapes and buildings, whether historic or those created today, still influence us. They still express cultural, social, and religious ideologies. They still unite and unify people around a common identity. Their location, placement on the landscape, architectural style, and design still shape us as individuals, as communities, and as societies. Similar to the past peoples of St. Paul's Parish, Cahaba, and Cane Hill, most of us are not cognizant of how much religious landscapes and buildings shape us.

When I was in the early stages of writing this book, Notre-Dame

Cathedral in Paris caught fire. One did not have to identify themselves as a parishioner, Catholic, Christian, or French to be affected by the damage—millions mourned the destruction of large portions of the world-famous cathedral. At least for a few days, people around the world united around a single religious structure and all that it symbolizes. They mourned the destruction to an architectural wonder, posted photographs of their visits to the cathedral on social media, donated money toward renovations, and expressed their sorrow for the loss of religious artifacts.

Over its 850-year history, Notre-Dame Cathedral has served as a symbol of many different things to many different people. From the time its construction began in 1163 and through several phases of construction over the next two centuries, Notre-Dame's extravagant French Gothic architectural style materially expressed the ideology, power, wealth, and influence of the Catholic Church and that of the French monarchy. During the French Revolution, resentment of the monarchy and the Church led to revolutionaries seizing the cathedral, destroying statues and other parts of the building, and renaming it. Instead of symbolizing the power, influence, and wealth of the Catholic Church and the French monarchy, the building became a symbol of the revolutionary movement and its victories. Returned to the Catholic Church in 1801 by Napoleon Bonaparte, Notre-Dame has since served as the backdrop for many important events and ceremonies, including Bonaparte's coronation as emperor, a celebratory mass after the liberation of France in the waning days of World War II, and requiem masses for French and Catholic leaders. For most of its existence, Notre-Dame has materially expressed both Catholic and French ideologies and identities. On the day of the 2019 fire, in a statement to the press French president Emmanuel Macron stated, "Notre-Dame is our history, our literature, part of our psyche, the place of all our great events, our epidemics, our wars, our liberations, the epicenter of our lives." Today, Notre-Dame Cathedral is a symbol of hope, and in the future, optimistically, the restored cathedral will be a symbol of renewal.

Even those religious structures and landscapes created more recently are still deliberately designed to express ideology and invoke meaning, not just to their respective followers but to others as well. The Washington, DC, Temple of the Church of Jesus Christ of Latter-day Saints is one such example. Opened in 1974, the temple has a "silent conversation with the outside world" about the Church of Jesus Christ, its ideology, its identity, and how they want nonmembers to perceive them (Leone 2010:105). Just as in the three historic case studies presented in this book, the people involved with the temple's design deliberately used architectural design and landscape to express their identity and to visually showcase their temple. Their goal was for their temple to "be a building of beauty, significance, and distinction" (Church of Jesus Christ of Latter-day Saints 1974). The finished product easily fulfills that goal. From its overall size of just under 15,000 sq. m, to the bright Alabama white marble exterior, to the 24-carat gold spires that stretch nearly 88 m in height, the temple is a visual showcase (Church of Jesus Christ of Latter-day Saints 1974). Temple designers also used the surrounding natural landscape to their advantage by placing the building on a hill, adding to its overall height. By far, the temple is the tallest and most visible structure for miles. It also sits immediately along the Capital Beltway that surrounds Washington, DC, and some of its closest suburbs. Every day, tens of thousands of people pass by the temple in their vehicles, and it is nearly impossible for them to miss the temple from the roadway (Figure E.1).

Through conscious decisions regarding the design of their Washington, DC temple and use of the natural and cultural landscapes, Latter-day Saints communicate several messages about their religious beliefs and their identity. These messages include that they are indeed Christians, that the Church is wealthy and organized, and that they are gaining more power and influence. In particular, their presence in the Mid-Atlantic East Coast expresses

FIGURE E.1. Washington, DC, Temple of the Church of Jesus Christ of Latter-day Saints, Kensington, Maryland, as seen from the Capital Beltway, 2007. (Photograph by IFCAR.)

how their influence and membership have grown enough to spread their message beyond Utah and the West. Additionally, by constructing their temple in the Washington, DC, metropolitan area, they materially expressed that they had gained enough power and influence nationally to secure a place in the nation's capital (Leone 2010:105).

Religious landscapes are found throughout today's southeastern United States, with churches and other places of worship as the most recognizable and numerous. From quaint, rural churches that hold only a handful of worshippers to urban megachurches that hold thousands of worshippers, these structures, along with other types of religious landscapes, continue to serve as material expressions of ideologies and goals of the religious organization. More often than not, those ideologies and goals are also reflective of those of the larger community to which they belong. Similar to St. Paul's Parish Church, St. Luke's Episcopal Church, and Cane Hill College, modern religious landscapes also communicate messages about the ideology, goals, and identity—of their respective religious organization, the leaders who played a role in their design, and those of their followers. Beyond that, religious landscapes also invoke memories and feelings, which vary depending on own religious affiliations, or lack of one. Finally, they continue to create and reinforce social identities and very much remain a part of Southeastern identity.

Notes

CHAPTER 2

1. I alternate between spellings, based on the town's spelling for the period being discussed. Therefore, I use Cahawba when referring to the town when it served as the state capitol (through 1826) and Cahaba for the time after 1826.

2. A more detailed historical overview of Governor William Bibb, Cahawba's founding, and its early years as the state capitol can be found in *Three Capitals: A Book about the First Three Capitals of Alabama*, by William H. Brantley (1976), *Cahaba: Hallowed Ground* by John Scott, and *The Formative Period of Alabama, 1815–1828* by Thomas Perkins Abernathy (1965).

CHAPTER 3

1. Since its founding, Cane Hill has undergone several name changes, as witnessed by changes to the town's post office name. These names include Steam Mill, Boonsborough, Canehill, and Boonsboro, the name of the town for most of the nineteenth century. While today Cane Hill refers to the town proper, when the Cumberland Presbyterians and other white settlers first arrived in the region, Cane Hill referred to a larger area that spanned an approximately seven-mile ridge, including today's Canehill and Clyde communities. For simplicity and continuity, I use Cane Hill when referring to the physical town itself and its surrounding community, as that is the spelling Historic Cane Hill Inc. uses.

2. For a more in-depth examination of Cumberland Presbyterian Church history, see *A People Called Cumberland Presbyterian*, by Barrus, Baughn, and Campbell (1972). Overviews of Cumberland Presbyterians in Arkansas can be found in *Arkansas Cumberland Presbyterians 1812–1984* by Campbell (1985) and *Cumberland Presbyterians in Northwest Arkansas, 1827–1865* by Gage (2006).

References Cited

Abernathy, Thomas Perkins
    1965   *The Formative Period of Alabama, 1815–1828.* Brown Printing Company, Montgomery, Alabama.

Ali, Jason R., and Peter Cunich
    2005   The Church East and West: Orientating the Queen Anne Churches, 1711–34. *Journal of the Society of Architectural Historians* 64(1):56–73.

Anderson, Benedict
    1991   *Imagined Communities: Reflections on the Origins and Spread of Nationalism.* Verso, London.

Arendt, Beatrix
    2011   *Gods, Goods, and Big Game: The Archaeology of Labrador Inuit Choices in an Eighteenth- and Nineteenth-Century Mission Context.* PhD dissertation, Department of Anthropology, University of Virginia, Charlottesville.

Arkansas State Legislature
    1850   An Act to Incorporate the Cane Hill Collegiate Institute, Little Rock, Arkansas, December 26, 1850.
    1852a   An Act to Incorporate Cane Hill College, Little Rock, Arkansas, December 15, 1852.
    1852b   An Act to Incorporate Cane Hill Female Seminary, Little Rock, Arkansas, December 10, 1852.

Auburn University Rural Studio (website)
    2022a   St. Luke's Church—Phase 1.
    2022b   St. Luke's Church—Phase 2.

Barrus, Ben Melton, Milton L. Baughn, and Thomas H. Campbell
    1972   *A People Called Cumberland Presbyterians.* Frontier Press, Memphis.

Basham, Robert Harold
    1969   *A History of Cane Hill College in Arkansas.* EdD dissertation, College of Education, University of Arkansas. University Microfilms, Ann Arbor.

Baugher, Sherene, and Richard F. Veit
    2014   *The Archaeology of American Cemeteries and Gravemarkers.* University Press of Florida, Gainesville.

Bentham, Jeremy
    1962   *The Works of Jeremy Bentham*, edited by John Bowring, Volume 4. Russell & Russell, New York.

References Cited

Bolton, Charles S.
    1971   South Carolina and the Reverend Doctor Francis Le Jau: Southern Society and the Conscience of an Anglican Missionary. *Historical Magazine of the Protestant Episcopal Church* 40(1):63–79.
    1982   *Southern Anglicanism: The Church of England in Colonial South Carolina.* Greenwood Press, Westport, Connecticut.

Braly, Bobby R.
    2019   *Images of America: Cane Hill.* Arcadia Publishing, Charleston, South Carolina.
    2020   Photographs Offer Glimpse into Life in Historical Cane Hill. *Flashback* 70(1):2–12.

Brantley, William H.
    1976   *Three Capitals: A Book about the First Three Capitals of Alabama.* University of Alabama Press, Tuscaloosa.

Bromberg, Francine W., and Steven J. Shephard
    2006   The Quaker Burying Ground in Alexandria, Virginia: A Study of Burial Practices of the Religious Society of Friends. *Historical Archaeology* 40(1):57–88.

Brooke, Christopher J.
    1986   Ground-based Remote Sensing for the Archaeological Study of Churches. In *The Anglo-Saxon Church: Papers on History, Architecture, and Archaeology in Honour of Dr. H. M. Taylor,* edited by L. A. S. Butler and R. K. Morris, pp. 210–217. Research Report 60. Council for British Archaeology, London.

Cahaba Advisory Committee
    2017   St. Luke's Church.

Caldwell, Ronald J.
    1997   A History of Saint Luke's Episcopal Church, Cahaba, Alabama. Manuscript on file, Old Cahawba Archaeological Park, Orrville, Alabama.

Campbell, Thomas H.
    1985   *Arkansas Cumberland Presbyterians, 1812–1984: A People of Faith.* Arkansas Synod of the Cumberland Presbyterian Church, Memphis.

Cane Hill College
    1859   *The First Annual Catalogue of the Officers and Students in Cane Hill College, at Boonsboro, Arkansas, for the Academic Year 1858.* Times Office, Fort Smith, Arkansas.
    1877   *Catalogue of Cane Hill College, Cane Hill, Ark. for the Scholastic Year 1876-7.* Arkansas Sentinel Job Print, Fayetteville, Arkansas.

Carmichael, David, Jane Hubert, and Brian Reeves
    1994   Introduction. In *Sacred Sites, Sacred Places,* edited by David L. Carmichael, Jane Hubert, Brian Reeves, and Audhild Schance, pp. 1–8. Routledge, New York.

Carnahan, Reverend Alfred E.
    1954   *The Pyeatts and the Carnahans of Old Cane Hill.* Washington County Historical Society Bulletin Series #8. Fayetteville, Arkansas.

Casey, Edward S.
    2008   Place in Landscape Archaeology. In *Handbook of Landscape Archaeology,* edited by Bruno David and Julian Thomas, pp. 44–50. Left Coast Press, Walnut Creek, California.

Chang, K. C.
    1968   Toward a Science of Prehistoric Society. In *Settlement Archaeology,* edited by K. C. Chang, pp. 1–9. National Press Books, Palo Alto, California.

Chenoweth, John M.
    2021   "In the Beginning was the Word": Religious Communities, Religious Landscapes. *Historical Archaeology* 55(4):435–443.

Church of Jesus Christ of Latter-day Saints
    1974   To Build a Temple. *Ensign*, August 1974.

Cohen, Anthony
    1985   *The Symbolic Construction of Community*. Tavistock Publications, London.

Committee on War Claims
    1880   Cane Hill College, Arkansas Report. House of Representatives 46th Congress, 2nd Session. Report No. 1468.

Cooper, Thomas
    1837   *The Statues at Large of South Carolina, Volume II*. A. S. Johnston, Columbia, South Carolina.

Crass, David Colin, and Richard D. Brooks
    1997   Settlement Patterning on an Agriculturally Marginal Landscape. In *Carolina's Historical Landscape: Archaeological Perspectives*, edited by Linda F. Stine, Martha Zierden, Lesley M. Drucker, and Christopher Judge, pp. 71–84. University of Tennessee Press, Knoxville.

Cushman, George F.
    1854   Consecration of St. Luke's. *The Spirit of Missions* 19:251–254.
    1855   Cahaba. *The Spirit of Missions* 20:148.

Dalcho, Frederick
    1820   *An Historical Account of the Protestant Episcopal Church in South Carolina*. E. Thayer, Charleston, South Carolina.

Dallas Gazette
    1854   "Description of St. Luke's Episcopal Church." 31 March. Selma, Alabama.

De Cunzo, L., and J. H. Ernstein
    2006   Landscapes, Ideology and Experience in Historical Archaeology. In *The Cambridge Companion to Historical Archaeology*, edited by D. Hicks and M. C. Beaudry, pp. 255–270. Cambridge University Press, Cambridge.

De Cunzo, Lu Ann, Therese O'Malley, Michael J. Lewis, George E. Thomas, and Christa Wilmanns-Wells
    1996   Father Rapp's Garden at Economy: Harmony Society Culture in Microcosm. In *Landscape Archaeology, Reading and Interpreting the American Historical Landscape*, edited by Rebecca Yamin and Karen Bescherer Metheny, pp. 91–114. University of Tennessee Press, Knoxville.

Deagan, Kathleen A.
    2013   The Historical Archaeology of Sixteenth-Century La Florida. *Florida Historical Quarterly* 92(3):349–374.

Deetz, James
    1990   Prologue: Landscapes as Cultural Statements. In *Earth Patterns: Essays in Landscape Archaeology*, edited by William Kelso and Rachel Most, pp. 1–4. University Press of Virginia, Charlottesville.

Delle, James A.
    1998   *An Archaeology of Social Space: Analyzing Coffee Plantations in Jamaica's Blue Mountains*. Plenum Press, New York.

1999 The Landscapes of Class Negotiation on Coffee Plantations in the Blue Mountains of Jamaica: 1790–1850. *Historical Archaeology* 33(1):136–158.

DeMarrais, Elizabeth
2004 The Materialisation of Culture. In *Rethinking Materiality: The Engagement of Mind with the Material World*, edited by Elizabeth DeMarrais, Chris Gosden, and Colin Renfrew, pp. 11–22. McDonald Institute for Archaeological Research, Cambridge, England.

DeMarrais, Elizabeth, Luis Jaime Castillo, and Timothy Earle
1996 Ideology, Materialization, and Power Strategies. *Current Anthropology* 37(1):15–31.

DeMarrais, Elizabeth, Chris Gosden, and Colin Renfrew
2004 Introduction. In *Rethinking Materiality: The Engagement of Mind with the Material World*, edited by Elizabeth DeMarrais, Chris Gosden, and Colin Renfrew, pp. 1–25. McDonald Institute for Archaeological Research, Cambridge, England.

DePratter, Chester B., and Stanley South
1990 *Charlesfort: The 1989 Search Project*. Research Manuscript Series 221. South Carolina Institute of Archaeology and Anthropology, University of South Carolina, Columbia.

Derry, Linda
1997 Pre-Emancipation Archaeology: Does It Play in Selma, Alabama? *Historical Archaeology* 31(3):18–26.
2000 Southern Town Plans Storytelling, and Historical Archaeology. In *Archaeology of Southern Urban Landscapes*, edited by Amy Young, pp. 14–29. University of Alabama Press, Tuscaloosa.
2012 Old Cahawba. *Alabama Heritage* 103:33.

Doran, Susan, and Christopher Durston
2003 *Princes, Pastors, and People: The Church and Religion in England, 1500–1700*. Routledge, New York.

Droogan, Julian
2013 *Religion, Material Culture, and Archaeology*. Bloomsbury, London.

Ellis, David B.
1991 *The Presbyterians of Cane Hill, Arkansas*. ARC Press of Cane Hill, Arkansas.

Epperson, Terrence W.
1990 Race and the Disciplines of the Plantation. *Historical Archaeology* 24(4):6–10.
2004 Critical Race Theory and the Archaeology of the African Diaspora. *Historical Archaeology* 38(1):101–108.

Fitts, Robert K.
1999 The Archaeology of Middle-Class Domesticity and Gentility in Victorian Brooklyn. *Historical Archaeology* 33(1):39–62.

Foucault, Michel
1979 *Discipline and Punish*. Random House, New York.

Frankenburg, Ruth
1993 *White Women, Race Matters: The Social Construction of Whiteness*. University of Minnesota Press, Minneapolis.

Fry, Anna M. Gayle
1905 *Memories of Old Cahaba*. Publishing House of the Methodist Episcopal Church, South, Nashville.

Gage, Justin Randolph
    2006   Cumberland Presbyterians in Northwest Arkansas, 1827–1865. Master's thesis, Department of History, University of Arkansas, Fayetteville.

Gilchrist, Roberta
    2014   Monastic and Church Archaeology. *Annual Review of Anthropology* 43:235–250.

Gorsline, Meg
    2015   An Archaeology of Accountability: Recovering and Interrogating the "Invisible" Race. In *The Archaeology of Race in the Northeast*, edited by Christopher N. Matthews and Allison Manfra McGovern, pp. 291–310. University Press of Florida, Gainesville.

Greer, Georgeanna H.
    1981   *American Stonewares: The Art and Craft of Utilitarian Potters*. Schiffer Publishing, Atglen, Pennsylvania.

Gundersen, Joan R.
    1987   Rural Gothic: Episcopal Churches on the Minnesota Frontier. *Minnesota History* 50(7):258–268.

Harpole, Thane, David Brown, Mark Kostro, and Sarah Heimsman
    2007   *In the Shadow of Greatness: An Investigation of the 1670 Church at Historic Christ Church, Site 44LA55, Lancaster County, Virginia*. DATA Investigations. Submitted to Camille Bennett, Director, Foundation for Historic Christ Church, Irvington, Virginia.

Hartley, Michael O.
    1984   *The Ashley River: A Survey of Seventeenth Century Sites*. Research Manuscript Series 192. South Carolina Institute of Archaeology and Anthropology, University of South Carolina, Columbia.

Hawkins, Harriette.
    1983   *Icons in the Wilderness: The Anglican Churches of Rural South Carolina*. Master's thesis, University of Delaware, Newark. University Microfilms International, Ann Arbor, Michigan.

Heath, Barbara J.
    2007   Thomas Jefferson's Landscape of Retirement. In *Estate Landscapes: Design, Improvement and Power in the Post-Medieval Landscape*, edited by Jonathan Finch and Kate Giles, pp. 129–147. Boydell Press, Woodbridge, Suffolk, England.
    2010   Space and Place within Plantation Quarters in Virginia, 1700–1825. In *Cabin, Quarter, Plantation: Architecture and Landscapes of North American Slavery*, edited by Clifton Ellis and Rebecca Ginsburg, pp. 156–176. Yale University Press, New Haven, Connecticut.

Heath, Barbara, and Lori Lee
    2010   Memory, Race, and Place. *History Compass* 8(12):1352–1368.

Historic American Buildings Survey
    1936   St. Luke's Episcopal Church, (Moved from Cahaba, AL), Martin, Dallas County, AL. Library of Congress Prints and Photographs Division.

hooks, bell
    1990   *Yearning: Race, Gender, and Cultural Politics*. South End Press, Boston.

Hurry, Silas
    2011   Recreating the Chapel Historic St. Mary's City Archaeology, St. Mary's City, Maryland, website.

References Cited

Ingold, Tim
    2012   The Shape of the Land. In *Landscapes beyond Land: Routes, Aesthetics, Narratives*, edited by Arnar Arnason, Nicolas Ellison, Jo Vergunst, and Andrew Whitehouse, pp. 197–208. Berghahn Books, New York.

Isbell, William H.
    2000   What We Should Be Studying. In *The Archaeology of Communities: A New World Perspective*, edited by Marcello A. Canuto and Jason Yaeger, pp. 243–266. Routledge, New York.

Johnson, Matthew
    2006   *Ideas of Landscape*. Wiley-Blackwell, Malden, Massachusetts.

Joseph, J. W., and Martha Zierden
    2002   Cultural Diversity in the Southern Colonies. In *Another's Country: Archaeological and Historical Perspectives on Cultural Interactions in the Southern Colonies*, edited by J. W. Joseph and Martha Zierden, pp. 1–12. University of Alabama Press, Tuscaloosa.

Karnes, Wanda
    1985   Cane Hill College. In *A History of Cane Hill College*, edited by Conrow R. Miller, Cane Hill, Arkansas.

Knight, Vernon James, Jr.
    1987   A Report of Alabama DeSoto Commission/Alabama State Museum of Natural History Archaeological Test Excavations at the Site of Old Cahawba, Dallas County, Alabama. University of Alabama, Tuscaloosa.

Kruczek-Aaron, Hadley
    2015   *Everyday Religion: An Archaeology of Protestant Belief and Practice in the Nineteenth Century*. University Press of Florida, Gainesville.

Kryder-Reid, Elizabeth
    1994   As Is the Gardener, So Is the Garden: The Archaeology of Landscape as Myth. In *Historical Archaeology of the Chesapeake*, edited by Paul Shackel and Barbara Little, pp. 131–148. Smithsonian Institution Press, Washington, DC.
    1996   The Construction of Sanctity: Landscape and Ritual in a Religious Community. In *Landscape Archaeology: Reading and Interpreting the American Historical Landscape*, edited by Rebecca Yamin and Karen Bescherer Metheny, pp. 228–248. University of Tennessee Press, Knoxville.

Lane, Jack C.
    2012   Florida's Carpenter Gothic Churches: Artistic Gems from a Victorian Past. *The Florida Historical Quarterly* 91(2):248–270.

Lemke, W. J. (editor)
    1955   Session Minutes of the Cumberland Presbyterian Church, Cane Hill, Arkansas 1828–1843. Washington County Historical Society Bulletin Series Number 12. Fayetteville, Arkansas.

Lenik, Stephan
    2010   *Frontier Landscapes, Missions, and Power: A French Jesuit Plantation and Church at Grand Bay, Dominica (1747–1763)*. PhD dissertation, Department of Anthropology, Syracuse University, New York.
    2011   Mission Plantations, Space, and Social Control: Jesuits as Planters in French Caribbean Colonies and Frontiers. *Journal of Social Archaeology* 12(1):51–71.

Leone, Mark P.
    1984   Interpreting Ideology in Historical Archaeology: Using the Rules of Perspective in the

William Paca Garden in Annapolis, Maryland. In *Ideology, Power and Prehistory*, edited by Daniel Miller and Christopher Tilley, pp. 25–36. Cambridge University Press, Cambridge.
   2005   *The Archaeology of Liberty in an American City: Excavations in Annapolis*. University of California Press, Berkeley.
   2010   *Critical Historical Archaeology*. Left Coast Press, Walnut Creek, California.

Leone, Mark, James M. Harmon, and Jessica L. Neuwirth
   2005   Perspective and Surveillance in Eighteenth-Century Maryland Gardens, Including William Paca's Garden on Wye Island. *Historical Archaeology* 39(4):131–150.

Lewis, Kenneth
   1984   *The American Frontier: An Archaeological Study of Settlement Pattern and Process*. Academic Press, Orlando.

Linder, Suzanne Cameron
   2000   *Anglican Churches in Colonial South Carolina: Their History and Architecture*. Wyrick and Company, Charleston, South Carolina.

Lipsitz, George
   1995   The Possessive Investment in Whiteness: Racialized Social Democracy and the "White" Problem in American Studies. *American Quarterly* 47(3):369–387.

Low, Setha M., and Denise Lawrence-Zúñiga
   2003   Locating Culture. In *The Anthropology of Space and Place*, edited by Setha M. Low and Denise Lawrence-Zúñiga, pp. 1–47. Blackwell Publishing, Malden, Massachusetts.

Lydon, Jane
   2009   *Fantastic Dreaming: The Archaeology of an Aboriginal Mission*. AltaMira Press, Lanham, Maryland.

McAlester, Virginia, and Lee McAlester
   2000   *A Field Guide to American Houses*. Alfred A. Knopf, New York.

McCulloch, Lacy P.
   1989   *History of Cane Hill College in Pictures and Words*. ARC Press of Cane Hill, Cane Hill, Arkansas.

McDonnold, B. W.
   1888   *History of the Cumberland Presbyterian Church*. Board of Publication of the Cumberland Presbyterian Church, Nashville.

McKee, Harley J.
   1973   *Introduction to Early American Masonry, Stone, Brick, Mortar, and Plaster*. Preservation Press, Washington, DC.

McNair, Stephen
   2015   Richard Upjohn's Gothic Revival in Antebellum Alabama. *Alabama Heritage* 116:10–21.
   2017   Richard Upjohn and the Gothic Revival in Antebellum Alabama. In *Gothic Revival Worldwide: A. W. N. Pugin's Global Influence*, edited by Timothy Brittain-Catlin, Jan De Maeyer, and Martin Bressani, pp. 106–117. Leuven University Press, Leuven, Belgium.

Miller, Conrow R., and Gregory R. Williams
   1969   *The Cane Hill Story 1825–1969*. ARC Press of Cane Hill, Arkansas.

Moir, Randall W.
   1983   Windows to Our Past: A Chronological Scheme for the Thickness of Pane Fragments from 1635–1982. Manuscript, Corning Museum of Glass, Corning, New York.

Morgan, Philip
    1998   *Slave Counterpoint: Black Culture in the Eighteenth-Century Chesapeake and Lowcountry.* University of North Carolina Press, Chapel Hill.

Morris, Annelise
    2017   Materialities of Homeplace. *Historical Archaeology* 51:28–52.

Morris, Richard
    1983   *The Church in British Archaeology.* Research Report No. 47. Council for British Archaeology, London.
    1989   *Churches in the Landscape.* J. M. Dent and Sons, London.

National Oceanic and Atmospheric Administration (NOAA)
    2012   Magnetic Field Calculators. National Geophysical Data Center.

National Register of Historic Places
    1976   St. James Church, Goose Creek, Berkeley County, South Carolina, National Register #70000581.

Neill, Stephen
    1958   *Anglicanism.* Penguin, New York.

Nelson, Louis P.
    2001   *The Material Word: Anglican Visual Culture in Colonial South Carolina.* PhD dissertation, Department of Art History, University of Delaware.
    2008   *The Beauty of Holiness: Anglicanism and Architecture in Colonial South Carolina.* University of North Carolina Press, Chapel Hill.
    2009   The Diversity of Countries: Anglican Churches in Virginia, South Carolina, and Jamaica. In *Material Culture in Anglo-American: Regional Identity and Urbanity in the Tidewater, Lowcountry, and Caribbean,* edited by David S. Shields, pp. 74–101. University of South Carolina Press, Columbia.

Oatis, Steven J.
    2004   *A Colonial Complex: South Carolina's Frontiers in the Era of the Yamasee War, 1680–1730.* University of Nebraska Press, Lincoln.

Orser, Charles E., Jr.
    2007   *The Archaeology of Race and Racialization in Historic America.* University Press of Florida, Gainesville.

Patterson, Thomas C.
    2008   A Brief History of Landscape Archaeology in the Americas. In *Handbook of Landscape Archaeology,* edited by Bruno David and Julian Thomas, pp. 77–84. Left Coast Press, Walnut Creek, California.

Pauls, Elizabeth P.
    2006   The Place of Space: Architecture, Landscape, and Social Life. In *Historical Archaeology,* edited by Martin Hall and Stephen W. Silliman, pp. 65–83. Blackwell Publishing, Malden, Massachusetts.

Perrin, Richard W. E.
    1961   Richard Upjohn, Architect: Anglican Chapels in the Wilderness. *Wisconsin Magazine of History* 45(1):40–43.

Poplin, Eric, and Connie Huddleston
    1998   *Archaeological Data Recovery of the Thomas Lynch Plantation (38CH1479 and 38CH1585) RiverTowne Development Tract, Charleston County, South Carolina Volume 1: Final Report.* Brockington and Associates, Inc. Submitted to Wild Dunes Real

Estate, Mount Pleasant, South Carolina. Copies available from Brockington and Associates, Inc., Mount Pleasant.

Proebsting, Eric, and Jack Gary
    2016   Contributing to the Archaeology of American Landscapes. *Historical Archaeology* 50(1):1–6.

Protestant Episcopal Church, Diocese of Alabama
    1839   *Journal of the Proceedings of the Twenty-Second Annual Convention of the Protestant Episcopal Church in the Diocese of Alabama.* Morning Chronicle Print, Mobile, Alabama.
    1853   *Journal of the Proceedings of the Twenty-Second Annual Convention of the Protestant Episcopal Church in the Diocese of Alabama.* Benjamin, Jeter, and Co., Mobile, Alabama.
    1854   *Journal of the Proceedings of the Twenty-Second Annual Convention of the Protestant Episcopal Church in the Diocese of Alabama.* Benjamin, Farrow, and Co., Mobile, Alabama.

Pyszka, Kimberly
    2012   *"Unto Seytne Paules": Anglican Landscapes and Colonialism in South Carolina.* PhD dissertation, Department of Anthropology, University of Tennessee, Knoxville.

Pyszka, Kimberly, Bobby R. Braly, and Jamie Brandon
    2018   The Methodist "Manse" of Cane Hill: A New History. *Arkansas Historical Quarterly* 77(3):250–265.

Pyszka, Kimberly, Maureen Hays, and Scott Harris
    2010   The Archaeology of St. Paul's Parish Church, Hollywood, South Carolina, USA. *Journal of Church Archaeology* 12:71–78.

Ramsey, William L.
    2008   *The Yamasee War: A Study of Culture, Economy, and Conflict in the Colonial South.* University of Nebraska Press, Lincoln.

Richardson, Ellen Earle
    1955   *Early Settlers of Cane Hill.* Washington County Historical Society Bulletin Series #9. Fayetteville, Arkansas.

Roark, Randal
    1985   Old Cahawba: The Antebellum Town as Artifact. *Southeastern College Art Conference Review* 10(5):265–271.

Rodman, Margaret C.
    2003   Empowering Place: Multilocality and Multivocality. In *The Anthropology of Space and Place*, edited by Setha M. Low and Denise Lawrence-Zúñiga, pp. 204–223. Blackwell, Malden, Massachusetts.

Rodwell, Warwick
    2005   *The Archaeology of Churches.* Tempus Publishing Limited, Stroud, England.

Rosman, Doreen
    2003   *The Evolution of the England Churches 1500–2000.* Cambridge University Press, Cambridge, England.

Ryden, Kent C.
    1993   *Mapping the Invisible Landscape, Folklore, Writing and the Sense of Place.* University of Iowa Press, Iowa City.

Scharfenberger, Gerard P.

2009   Upon This Rock: Salvage Archaeology at the Early-Eighteenth-Century Homdel Baptist Church. *Historical Archaeology* 43(1):12–29.

Schoen, Christopher M.
1990   Window Glass on the Plains: An Analysis of Flat Glass Samples from Ten Nineteenth Century Plains Historic Sites. *Central Plains Archaeology* 2(1):57–90.

Scott, John
2011   Cahaba: Hallowed Ground. *Alabama Heritage* 99:12–23.

Silver, Peter
2008   *Our Savage Neighbors: How Indian War Transformed Early America*. W. W. Norton and Company, New York.

Sipes, Eric, and Linda Derry
2019   A Capitol Set in the Wildness: Public Archaeology at Alabama's First Statehouse. Poster presented at the 76th Annual Meeting of the Southeastern Archaeological Conference, Jackson, Mississippi.

Smith, Ryan
1995   Carpenter Gothic: The Voices of Episcopal Churches on the St. John's River. *El Escribano* 32:65–90.

Society for Historical Archaeology
2020   Bottle/Glass Colors. Available via the Society for Historical Archaeology website.

South, Stanley, and Michael Hartley
1980   *Deep Water and High Ground: Seventeenth Century Lowcountry Settlement*. Research Manuscript Series 166. South Carolina Institute of Archaeology/Anthropology, University of South Carolina, Columbia.

Stanton, Phoebe B.
1997   *The Gothic Revival & American Church Architecture: An Episode in Taste 1840–1856*. John Hopkins University Press, Baltimore.

Steward, Julian H.
1955   *Theory of Culture Change*. University of Illinois Press, Urbana.

Thomas, Samuel
1905   Documents concerning Reverend Samuel Thomas, 1702–1707. *South Carolina Historical and Genealogical Magazine* 1:21–55.

Treib, Marc
2009   Yes, Now I Remember: An Introduction. In *Spatial Recall: Memory in Architecture and Landscapes*, edited by Marc Treib, pp. x–xv. Routledge, New York.

Upjohn, Everand M.
1939   *Richard Upjohn Architect and Churchman*. Columbia University Press, New York.

Upjohn, Richard
1975 [c1852]   *Upjohn's Rural Architecture: Designs, Working Drawings and Specifications for a Wooden Church, and Other Rural Structures*. De Capo Press, New York.

Upton, Dell
1986   *Holy Things and Profane: Anglican Parish Churches in Colonial Virginia*. MIT Press, Cambridge, Massachusetts.

Veit, Richard F., Sherene B. Baugher, and Gerard P. Scharfenberger
2009   Historical Archaeology of Religious Sites and Cemeteries. *Historical Archaeology* 43(1):1–11.

Verkaaik, Oskar

2013 Religious Architecture: Anthropological Perspectives. In *Religious Architecture: Anthropological Perspectives*, edited by Oskar Verkaaik, pp. 7–24. Amsterdam University Press, Amsterdam, the Netherlands.

Vergunst, Jo, Andrew Whitehouse, Nicolas Ellison, and Arnar Arnason
2012 Introduction. In *Landscapes beyond Land: Routes, Aesthetics, Narratives*, edited by Arnar Arnason, Nicolas Ellison, Jo Vergunst, and Andrew Whitehouse, pp. 1–14. Berghahn, New York.

Ward, Jeanne A., and John McCarthy
2009 Tea in God's Light: An Analysis of Artifacts from the Friends Meetinghouse Site, Burlington, New Jersey. *Historical Archaeology* 43(1):30–45.

Weiland, Jonathan
2009 A Comparison and Review of Window Glass Analysis Approaches in Historical Archaeology. *Technical Briefs in Historical Archaeology* 4:29–40.

Willey, Gordon
1953 *Prehistoric Settlement Patterns in the Viru Valley, Peru*. Bureau of American Ethnology Bulletin 155. Washington, DC.

Winthrop, John
1630 A Model of Christian Charity. Available via the Winthrop Society website.

Woolverton, John Frederick
1984 *Colonial Anglicanism in North America*. Wayne State University Press, Detroit.

Yaeger, Jason, and Marcello A. Canuto
2000 Introducing an Archaeology of Communities. In *The Archaeology of Communities: A New World Perspective*, edited by Marcello A. Canuto and Jason Yaeger, pp. 1–15. Routledge, New York.

Yamin, Rebecca, and Karen Bescherer Metheny
1996 Preface: Reading the Historical Landscape. In *Landscape Archaeology: Reading and Interpreting the American Historical Landscape*, edited by Rebecca Yamin and Karen Bescherer Metheny, pp. xiii–xx. University of Tennessee Press, Knoxville.

Young, Amy L.
2000 Introduction: Urban Archaeology in the South. In *Archaeology of Southern Urban Landscapes*, edited by Amy L. Young, pp. 1–13. University of Alabama Press, Tuscaloosa.

Zierden, Martha
2002 Frontier Society in South Carolina: An Example from Willtown (1690–1800). In *Another's Country: Archaeological and Historical Perspectives on Cultural Interactions in the Southern Colonies*, edited by J. W. Joseph and Martha Zierden, pp. 181–197. University of Alabama Press, Tuscaloosa.

Zierden, Martha, Suzanne Linder, and Ron Anthony
1999 *Willtown: An Archaeological and Historical Perspective*. The Charleston Museum Archaeological Contributions 27, South Carolina Department of Archives and History, Columbia.

Zierden, Martha, and Linda Stine
1997 Introduction: Historical Landscapes through the Prism of Archaeology. In *Carolina's Historical Landscape: Archaeological Perspectives*, edited by Linda F. Stine, Martha Zierden, Lesley M. Drucker, and Christopher Judge, pp. xi–xvi. University of Tennessee Press, Knoxville.

Index

African Methodist Episcopal (AME) Church, 103
Africans, 99–100; and Christianization, 22. *See also* enslaved labor; enslaved peoples
aisles, as architectural feature, 36–37
Alabama, 104; bicentennial of statehood, 47–48, 69; Episcopal churches, 59, 62; Gothic Revival churches, 63. *See also* St. Luke's Episcopal Church
Alabama, Episcopalian Diocese of, 52, 61
Alabama Historical Commission (AHC), 47–48, 51–52, 69
Alabama River, 17, 49, 61, 65–70, 102
Alabama State Museum of Natural History, Expedition program, 66
Alabama Territory, General Assembly, 49–50
alcohol consumption, 88–89
Ali, Jason R., 28
altar, as focal point of interior space, 57
altar table, 40
Anglican Church, 3, 11–12, 15–16, 19–46, 49, 58, 90–91, 96–101; canon law, 28, 97; and Catholic influence, 40; establishment of, in Carolina Colony, 43; and Gothic Revival architecture, 56–57. *See also* Protestant Episcopal Church (denomination); St. Paul's Parish Church
Anglican churches, in South Carolina, 5, 11, 17, 20, 22, 28–34, 40, 97–98, 100–102
Annapolis, Maryland, 9, 90–91
archaeological surveys/excavations, 4–5; at Cahaba, 65–67; at Cane Hill, 81–89; at St. Luke's Episcopal Church, 48, 65–67; at St. Paul's Parish Church, 34–39
architectural artifacts, at Cane Hill, 83–89
architectural debris, 37–38; at Cane Hill, 84–85
architectural information, 4–5
architectural separation, between nave and chancel, 36–37, 39
architectural studies, 8–13
archival research, 4–5
Arkansas, 4, 15, 17–18, 75–76, 105; Arkansas State Legislature, 76. *See also* Cane Hill, Arkansas; Cane Hill College
Arkansas Cumberland College, Clarksville (later University of the Ozarks), 80
Arkansas Synod (Cumberland Presbyterian), 76–77
artifact analysis, 4–5; at Cane Hill, 83–88; St. Paul's Parish Church, 29, 37–38
artifact assemblages: from church sites, 7–8; from domestic sites, 87
artifact distribution, at Cane Hill, 83, 85–87
ash layer, at Cane Hill, 84–85
Ashley River, 21, 29, 33
auditory experience, in church service, 58
Azion Baptist Church, 54

baptismal font, 40
Baptists, 52, 54
barrel-vaulted ceiling, 39
Beaufort, South Carolina, 21
Beaufort River, 32–33

Bellinger, Landgrave Edmund, 23, 29, 45, 99
Bentham, Jeremy, 91
Bibb, Governor William Wyatt, 49–50, 67
"Bible Belt," use of term, 107
biblical citations: Ezekiel 43:2, 28; Matthew 24:27, 28
"Black Belt" (Central Alabama), 50
Black community: Baptist congregation, 54; at Cahaba, 103–104; and racial separation, 61–63, 102–104. *See also* Africans; enslaved labor; enslaved peoples; racial segregation; slavery
Blake, Governor Joseph, 45
Blount, Brigadier General James, 77–78
board-and-batten siding, 54, 61
Braly, Bobby R., 82
brick fragments, 82–84
bricks, 8, 57, 59, 61; glazed, 37–39; handmade, 83
brickwork, 36
Bull, Reverend William, 23–24
buttresses, external, 55, 60

Cahaba/Cahawba, Alabama, 13–14, 16–17, 47–49, 58, 96, 113n1 (chap. 2); Black community of, 17, 103–104; community formation, 101–104; historical overview, 49–52; population, 51; school for children of Black tenant farmers, 103–104; St. Paul's AME Church, 103; St. Paul's Methodist Church, 103. *See also* St. Luke's Episcopal Church
Cahaba Foundation, 52
Cahaba River, 67
Cahawba Advisory Committee, 54
Calvinism, 74–75, 99
Cambridge Camden Society (Ecclesiological Society), 57
Cambridge University, 57
Cane Hill, Arkansas, 15, 17–18, 72–94, 96, 106; cemetery, 76, 89; focus on history and heritage, 18, 96, 106; name changes, 113n1 (chap. 3)
Cane Hill College (NW Arkansas), 3–5, 10–13, 15, 17–18, 72–94; archaeological excavations, 5, 81–89; artifact analysis, 83–88; and Civil War, 77–78; closures, 73, 80, 105; community formation, 104–106; curriculum, 79–80; dormitory, 77–78; fire, 80, 87, 90, 105; founding, 73; landscape use, 89–93; location, 81–89; merger with Cane Hill Female Seminary (1875), 79; postwar rebuilding, 78–80; public school, 80–81, 105–106; student body, 77–79; successive buildings, 74, 81–90; surviving structure (1886), 80–81, 90; various names, 77
Cane Hill College Association, 106
Cane Hill Collegiate Institute, 76–77, 90
Cane Hill Cumberland Presbyterian Church, 76; "White Church," 92
Cane Hill Female Seminary, 77; merger with Cane Hill College (1875), 79
Cane Hill School, 76–78, 89
Canuto, Marcello, 13
capitalism, rise of, 9
Carnahan, John, 75–76
Carnahan, Reverend Alfred E., 89
Carnahan family, 75–76
Carolina Colony, 21–25. *See also* South Carolina
Carpenter Gothic architecture, 49, 54, 59–61, 65
Castillo, Luis Jaime (DeMarrais et al. 1996), 10–11, 28, 33, 92–93, 96–97
Catholic Church, 56–57, 108–109
Catholic churches, 39
Catholic influence, 40, 56–57
centrality, and church location, 29, 71, 89
ceramics, 83, 87–88
chapels of ease, 24, 32–33
Charles II (king of England), 21
Charlesfort settlement, 21
Charleston, South Carolina, 21
Charles Towne settlement, 21, 23
choir area, 55
Christ Church Parish (South Carolina), 30
Christianization, 22, 100
church archaeology, in England, 6–7
church architecture: as backdrop for liturgy, 58; and materialization of ideology, 59–65; reflecting northeastern roots, 64. *See also* Carpenter Gothic architecture; Gothic Revival architecture; St. Luke's Episcopal Church; St. Paul's Parish Church; Upjohn, Richard

Index

church construction, significance of, 95–97
church design, 19–20, 34; and racial segregation, 61–63. *See also* church architecture
church furnishings, 40, 58
church height, 57. *See also* elevation, of religious site; verticality
church interior, 55, 57; capacity of, 39; dark, 58, 61; and natural light, 39, 60–61; racially segregated, 61–63; St. Luke's Episcopal Church, 60–61
Church of England. *See* Anglican Church
Church of Jesus Christ of Latter-day Saints, 109–111
churchyard studies, in England, 7
Civil War, US, 47, 51, 54, 77–78, 87, 89, 91, 102
Classical architecture, 57
Cobbs, Bishop, 54
College of Charleston, 34; Department of Sociology and Anthropology, 20; Stono River Preserve (Dixie Plantation), 25
commemorative plaque, for St. Paul's Parish Church, 20
Committee on War Claims, 78–79
communion, 37, 39
community, defining, 4
community formation, 46, 71, 93–107
community identity, 13–15
community studies, 13
Confederacy, 77, 105
container glass, 83, 87–89. *See also* window glass
conversion, religious, 22, 100
Cooper, Lord Anthony Ashley, 22
Cooper River, 32–33
cotton production, 50–51, 70, 104
Creek Indians, 49, 69
Creek War (1813–1814), 69
critical materialism, 9
critical race theory (CRT), 14–15
critical whiteness studies, 14–15
cruciform structure, 25, 37, 54–55
cultural ecology, 8
cultural identifiers, 13, 96
cultural landscapes, 1–3, 8, 34, 67–71
Cumberland Presbyterian Church (denomination), 3, 15, 17–18, 52, 72–94, 96, 105; denunciation of alcohol/tobacco use, 88–89; focus on behavior, 91–92; focus on education, 72–94, 105; historical overview, 74–81. *See also* Cane Hill College
Cumberland Presbytery (Presbyterian), 75
Cumming, David, 53, 60–62
Cunich, Peter, 28
Cushman, Reverend, 63

Dallas County, Alabama, 16, 50–52; courthouse, 69, 71. *See also* Cahaba/Cahawba, Alabama
dating, of window glass fragments, 83–84
decorative/ornamental features, emphasis on, in Gothic Revival style, 48–49, 54, 101–102
deep water and high ground model, 29, 32
deerskins, trade in, 21
Deetz, James, 2
DeMarrais, Elizabeth, 10–11, 28, 33, 92–93, 96–97
Derry, Linda, 16, 65–67
Dick, John Henry, burial of (1995), 27, 37
Dissenters, 16, 20–22, 33–34, 44, 96–101
documentary evidence, 5, 7, 38, 44, 65, 106
domestic sites, 33, 87
Dun, Reverend William, 34, 44

Earle, Fountain Richard, 77, 80, 88–89
Earle, Timothy (DeMarrais et al. 1996), 10–11, 28, 33, 92–93, 96–97
east-west orientation, of churches, 28, 97
education: as cultural identifier, 96, 105; Cumberland Presbyterian focus on, 72–94, 105
elevation, of religious site, 5, 30, 57
emancipation, 51, 102–103
England/English, 6–7, 11, 33, 39, 49, 97–101; Carolina settlements, 21; Charter of Carolina (1663), 21
enslaved labor, 4, 9, 15, 21, 33, 50–51. *See also* emancipation
enslaved peoples, and church attendance, 55, 62, 98, 100
entrances, 102; at St. Luke's Episcopal Church, 62; at St. Paul's Parish Church, 36–37
environmental conditions, for St. Luke's Episcopal Church, 61–62
Episcopal Church, 47–71. *See also* Protestant Episcopal Church (denomination); St. Luke's Episcopal Church

Episcopal churches: Alabama, 59, 62; Florida, 64–65; Minnesota, 59. *See also* St. Luke's Episcopal Church
Episcopalians, 52–54, 71
extant structures, study of, 5

Farr, Thomas, 23, 25, 44, 98
Federal architecture, 69
flooding, 29, 51, 54, 61
Florida: Episcopal churches in, 64–65; Spanish, 21
Foucault, Michel, 91
foundations: of St. Luke's Episcopal Church, 60–61; of St. Paul's Parish Church, 36
France/French, 33–34, 108–109; Carolina settlements, 21
Fraser, Charles, 43
free will, 74–75
fundraising, for church building, 52–53

geographic information systems (GIS), 7
Georgian architecture, 57
Goose Creek (tributary of Cooper River), 32–33
"Goose Creek Men," 43
Gothic architecture, 109
Gothic Revival architecture, 16, 48–49, 54–59, 64–65, 101
Grace Episcopal Church (Clayton, Alabama), 59
Grace Episcopal Church (Mt. Meigs, Alabama), 59
ground-penetrating radar (GPR), 5, 25, 27, 38
Gundersen, Joan R., 101–102
Guy, Reverend, 40

Harris, Scott, 25
Hartley, Michael, 29–30
Hawkins, Harriett, 11
Hicks, Hugh, 23, 25, 44, 98
High Church (Anglican), 22, 40, 43–44, 49, 56–59, 61, 101
high ground, and church placement, 29, 32
hilltop location, 90–93, 105, 110
Historic American Buildings Survey (HABS), 48, 64
Historic Cane Hill Inc., 72, 82, 106

history and heritage, as basis for identity, 18, 96, 106
"homeplace," 103–104
hooks, bell, 103
Huguenots, French, 99
Hunt, Brian, 45
Hunter, Judge William, 53, 60

ideational perspective, 13
identity: English, 22; racial, 14–15, 98, 100–104, 107; religious/social, 10, 98, 105; white Carolina, 22, 46. *See also* Black community; community formation; settlers, white
Indian trade, 23
Indigenous peoples, 3–4, 6, 20, 22, 33–34, 49, 99–100; and cultural landscape, 66–69
interactional perspective, 13

Johnson, Governor Nathanial, 22
Johnson, Matthew, 12

Kentucky, 75
Kentucky Synod (Presbyterian), 75
King, Reverend Samuel, 76
Ku Klux Klan, 103

landing area, 29–30
landscape, and materialization of ideology, 95–97
"land-scape," use of term, 12
landscape archaeology, 8–13
landscapes, religious, 32, 48; Cane Hill College, 81–93; modern examples, 108–111; St. Luke's Episcopal Church, 65–71; St. Paul's Parish Church, 25–30, 65
Le Lau, Reverend Francis, 43
Lenik, Stephan, 28
Leone, Mark, 9, 90–91
light, natural, 39, 60–61. *See also* windows
Lincoln School District (Arkansas), 81
lines of sight, 90–92
location, 29, 71; of Cane Hill College, 81–89; hilltop, 90–93, 105, 110 (*see also* elevation, of religious site); of St. Luke's Episcopal Church, 48, 54, 66–67, 102; of St. Paul's Parish Church, 26, 28–30

Index

Locke, John, 22
London, Anglican churches in, 28
Lords Proprietors (South Carolina), 21–22
Low Church (Anglican), 22, 40, 49, 56–57, 101
Lowry, Samuel Doak, 93
Ludlam, Reverend, 43
Lydon, Jane, 91

Macron, Emmanuel (president of France), 109
maps, 5; of Cahawba, 67–68
Martin's Station, Alabama, 54, 66
Marxism, 9
material culture, 6–8, 10–11, 15, 58, 101
materiality approach, 10–11
materialization of ideology, 10–11, 29–30, 33–34, 49, 59–71, 95–97, 108–111; Cane Hill College and, 81–89, 92–93, 106
McMahon, Robert T., 78
meeting house, at Cane Hill, 89
memorials, interior, 43
merchants, 52–53, 70
Methodist Episcopal Church, 80
Methodists, 52, 105
ministers: finding and keeping, 45; requirements for, 75, 92. *See also* names of individuals
ministry, Presbyterian, 75–76, 92
Minnesota, Episcopal churches in, 59
missionaries, 22–24, 43, 45, 98
Mitchell, Reverend, 53, 60
Mobile, Alabama, 58, 70
Moir, Randall W., 83–84
Montgomery, Alabama, 58, 70
Moravian Church, 91
Mormons, 109–111
Morris, Annelise, 103
mortar, 8

nails, 8, 83–87; roofing, 38
National Historic Preservation Act of 1966, Sec. 106, 7
Native Americans. *See* Indigenous peoples
Nelson, Louis, 11, 44
Nicholson, Governor Francis, 90–91
northeastern US roots, 64, 71
Notre-Dame Cathedral, Paris, 108–109

Old Cahawba, 16
Old Cahawba Archaeological Park, 47, 52, 54. *See also* Cahaba/Cahawba, Alabama
oral history, 82
orientation, of churches, 32; St. Luke's Episcopal Church, 66–67, 70; St. Paul's Parish Church, 25–28, 32
Oxford Movement, 56–57
Oxford University, 56

Paca, William, 9
panopticon, 91–92, 105
Perine, Edward, 53, 60
pew boxes, raised wooden, 36, 39
place, and space, defining, 12
planned town, Cahawba as, 67
plantation economy, 4, 104–105
planter houses, 33
planters, 43, 52. *See also* "Goose Creek Men"
plaster, 38–39, 55, 60–61
power, religious/social, 10; representation of, 69, 91, 97
practice theory, 13
predestination, Calvinist concept of, 74–75
prehistoric features, found at Cahawba, 66–67
Presbyterian Church, 93; Cumberland split from, 74. *See also* Cumberland Presbyterian Church (denomination)
Presbyterians, 20–21, 44, 52
preservation project, at Cane Hill, 72–74, 106
processual archaeology, 8–9
prohibition, 88–89
Protestant Episcopal Church (denomination), 3, 49, 101; affinity with Gothic Revival style, 56–59. *See also* St. Luke's Episcopal Church
Pugin, Augustus, 57
pulpit, 40, 57
Puritan influence, 39–40, 44, 90
purity, bodily, 88
Pyeatte family, 75

race, as cultural identifier, 14, 96. *See also under* identity
racial segregation, 49, 61–63, 102–104, 107
racial violence, 103
railings, wooden, 39

railroads, 50–51
Reformation, 39
religious diversity, in St. Paul's Parish, 44. *See also* Dissenters
religious ideology, expression of, 10; and St. Paul's Parish Church, 39–45. *See also* materialization of ideology
religious sites, study of, 5–8
religious tolerance, 40, 44; in Carolina Colony, 15, 22
remote sensing technology, 5. *See also* ground-penetrating radar (GPR)
reuse, of building materials, 24–25, 51
rice cultivation, 21, 23, 45, 104
Richardson, Ellen Earle, 89
Riordan, Tim, 36
roofs, wood-shingled, 38–39
rural churches, 40–41; and Carpenter Gothic style, 58–59

sacred places, 5–6
sacristy, 55
Saint Luke's Episcopal Church. *See* St. Luke's Episcopal Church
Saint Paul's Parish Church. *See* St. Paul's Parish Church
Salem Cumberland Presbyterian congregation, 76, 91–92
Santa Elena settlement, 21
satellite imagery, 5
Schoen, Christopher, 83–84
school, for children of Black tenant farmers, 103–104
Seabrook, Robert, 23, 25, 44, 98
Second Great Awakening, 74–75, 88
segregation. *See* racial segregation
Selma, Alabama, 51, 70
settlement archaeology, 9
settlements, European, 21
settlers, white, 20–21, 24, 33–34, 69, 98, 100
size, of church structure, 60, 63, 110
slate fragments, 87
slavery, 61–63, 107. *See also* Civil War, US; emancipation
Smith, Ryan, 64–65
social/cultural ideology, in church design, 61–63

Society for the Propagation of the Gospel in Foreign Parts (SPG), 22, 98
South, Stanley, 29–30
South Carolina, 11, 15–16, 21–22, 96–101, 104; Anglican churches, 5, 11, 17, 20, 22, 28–34, 40, 97–98, 100–102; Church Act (1706), 15, 19, 22–23, 30, 32; Fundamental Constitution (1669), 22; General Assembly, 19, 21–22, 32, 34, 40, 45, 98–99. *See also* St. Paul's Parish Church
Spain/Spanish, 33–34, 100; Carolina settlements, 21
spoken word, of religious leader, 58
stained glass, 38, 54–55, 58, 63–64, 70–71
St. Andrew's Episcopal Church (Prairieville, Alabama), 55, 59, 63
St. Andrew's Parish (South Carolina), 30, 44–45
St. Andrew's Parish Church (South Carolina), 32, 40
statehouse, planned, at Cahawba, 67–69
St. Augustine, Florida, 21, 24
St. Bartholomew's Parish (South Carolina), 30, 33
St. Denis Parish (Huguenot), 99
steps, as architectural feature, 39
St. George's Church (South Carolina), 32
St. George's Episcopal Church (Fort George Island, Florida), 64–65
St. Helena's Church (South Carolina), 32
St. Helena's Parish (South Carolina), 33
St. James's (Goose Creek) Parish (South Carolina), 30
St. James's (Goose Creek) Parish Church (South Carolina), 32–33, 42–44
St. James's (Santee) Parish (South Carolina), 30
St. John's (Berkeley) Parish (South Carolina), 30, 44–45
St. John's (Colleton) Parish, 24
St. John's Episcopal Church (Forkland, Alabama), 59
St. John's River, 64–65
St. Luke's Episcopal Church (Central Alabama), 3–5, 10–17, 47–71, 101–104; archaeological excavations, 48, 67–69; bell tower/spire, 48, 54, 60, 62, 70–71, 102;

Index

buttresses, 55, 60; and cultural landscape, 67–71; disassembly and reassembly, 54; environmental conditions, 61–62; floorplan, 54; gallery, 48, 55, 60–63, 102–104; interior, 55, 60–61; landscape, 65–71; and/as "materialization of ideology," 95–97; orientation, 66–67; original location, 66–67; overall dimensions, 60; and racial segregation, 61–63, 102–104; relocation, 48, 54; separate entrances, 62; and social/cultural ideology, 61–63; and verticality, 60–61; and visibility, 61, 65; visual appearance, 54; windows, 54–55, 60, 63–64, 70–71

St. Luke's Episcopal Church (Jacksonville, Alabama), 59

St. Luke's Parish (Alabama), 52, 54

St. Mary's Episcopal Church (Green Cove Springs, Florida), 64–65

stone, as building material, 57, 59, 61

Stono Rebellion (1739), 12, 100

Stono River, 23, 25, 28–29, 33, 45, 70, 97

St. Paul's AME Church (Cahaba, Alabama), 103

St. Paul's Episcopal Church (Lowndesboro, Alabama), 59

St. Paul's Episcopal Church (Magnolia Springs, Alabama), 59

St. Paul's Episcopal Church (Mobile, Alabama), 59

St. Paul's Methodist Church (Cahaba, Alabama), 103

St. Paul's Parish (South Carolina), 24, 30, 33, 45, 96; community formation, 97–101; population of, 24, 44, 100

St. Paul's Parish Church (South Carolina), 3–5, 10–13, 15–16, 19–46, 70; addition to, 24, 39; archaeological excavation, 5; architecture, 25, 34–39; capacity of structure, 39; cemetery, 25; dismantling of original building, 24–25; entrances, 36–37; floors, 36; landscape, 25–30, 65; location of, 26, 28–30; as "Low" church, 44, 98; and/as "materialization of ideology," 95–97; orientation, 25–28, 32; parsonage house, 23–24

St. Philip's Church (South Carolina), 40, 43–44

STPs (shovel-test pits), 83–85

Strawberry Chapel (South Carolina), 32, 37, 40–41, 44–45

St. Thomas's Parish (South Carolina), 30

stucco, 38, 40

Summerville, South Carolina, 20

temperance movement, 88–89

Temple of the Church of Jesus Christ of Latter-day Saints (Washington, DC), 109–111

Tennessee, 75

tobacco consumption, 88–89

town grids, 67

town map, of Cahawba, 67–68

trade networks, 7

transportation routes, 7

Transylvania Presbytery (Presbyterian), 75

trapezoidal structure, 69

Trinity Church (New York City), 58

truss arches, wooden, 55

Tuscaloosa, Alabama, 50

Union Army, 87

Union Church (Cahaba Church; Old Church), 52, 96, 102. *See also* St. Luke's Episcopal Church

United States Census: of 1860, 51; of 1870, 51

United States Geological Survey (USGS) maps, 26, 30

Upjohn, Richard, 58–59; "Wooden Church" plans, 58–64

Upton, Dell, 11

urban areas, and Gothic Revival architecture, 58

Vasser, A. M., 53, 60

Veit, Richard, 7

verticality, in Gothic Revival style, 48, 54–55, 60–61

Virginia, 11; churches, 36; militia, 24

visibility, of structures, 32–34, 57, 61, 65, 67–70, 92, 97

visual appearance of churches, 38–39, 54, 57

visual experience, in church service, 58

Washington, DC, 109–111

Washington County, Arkansas, 72, 76, 106
Washington Presbytery (Cumberland Presbyterian), 76–77
waterways: proximity to, 5, 29, 32, 65, 70; used as roads, 32–33, 70
wealth, of church members, 45, 52–53, 63, 102–103
Weiland, Jonathan, 83–84
Willey, Gordon, 8–9
window glass, 8, 38, 54–55, 83–87. *See also* stained glass

windows, 58, 63–64, 70–71; double, 60; lancet, 54–55
Winthrop, John, 90
wood, as building material, 59, 61
wooden tablets, hanging, 39–40
woodwork, interior, 43
Wren, Christopher, 40

Yaeger, Jason, 13
Yamasee Indian War (1715), 12, 23–24, 100
Yamasee people, 23